HABERMAS AND MARXISM

Volume 77, Sage Library of Social Research

Ⓢ Sage Library of Social Research

HABERMAS AND MARXISM

An Appraisal

Julius Sensat, Jr.

Volume 77
SAGE LIBRARY OF
SOCIAL RESEARCH

SAGE PUBLICATIONS   Beverly Hills   London

For information address:

SAGE PUBLICATIONS, INC.
275 South Beverly Drive
Beverly Hills, California 90212

SAGE PUBLICATIONS LTD
28 Banner Street
London EC1Y 8QE

Printed in the United States of America

International Standard Book Number 0-8039-1044-4

Library of Congress Cataloging in Publication Data

Sensat, Julius, 1947-
    Habermas and Marxism: an appraisal.

    (Sage library of social research ; v. 77)
    Bibliography: p. 169
    1. Marxian school of sociology. 2. Marxian economics.
    3. Habermas, Jürgen. I. Title.
HX56.S44   335.4   78-19847
ISBN 0-8039-1044-4
ISBN 0-8039-1045-2 pbk.

CONTENTS

To my father
and the memory of my mother

ACKNOWLEDGMENTS

Portions of previous drafts of this book were presented to various audiences at a number of universities: Ohio University, The University of Michigan, The University of Texas at Austin, Wichita State University, and The University of Wisconsin-Milwaukee. I am grateful for the constructive responses which I received at those places. A year-long study of Marx's *Capital* with a group at the Bread and Roses School in Austin, Texas was an important source of stimulation and clarification. The idea for the project goes back to several conversations with George Caffentzis, who stressed its importance as early as 1971. Some of the early work on the project was incorporated into my doctoral dissertation, submitted to the University of Texas in 1976. Helpful advice and criticism was provided during that stage by Edward Hewett, Robert Kane, Douglas Kellner, Alexander von Schoenborn, Robert Solomon, and especially Robert Palter. I also wish to thank the following persons who read portions of subsequent drafts and offered useful comments and suggestions: Christopher Ake, Douglas Booth, Oskar Negt, Kenneth Winkler, and especially Bernard Gendron, for many valuable conversations. Marc Linder, with whom I have collaborated in social-theoretic endeavors for several years, was enormously helpful at crucial points in the development of the project. Thanks are also due to Muriel Becker, Katherine Kirkish, and Jeffrey Williams for preparation of the manuscript, and to Lars Jensen of Sage Publications for his pleasant cooperation. Finally, for valuable advice on many matters, and for encouragement and support, I am especially grateful to Trudy Sensat.

A word on translations: Though I have referred whenever possible to English editions of originally German works, I have often modified the translations. Whenever I have done so, I have listed the German source in the bibliography.

Chapter 1

INTRODUCTION

The widespread and growing influence of Jürgen Habermas would suffice to justify a call for intellectuals on the left to make a serious effort to come to terms with his views. There is, however, another reason: his work represents a generally informed, quite systematic attempt to develop Marxist theory into a cogent, materially effective critique of contemporary capitalist society. This is not to say that there is nothing faulty or misguided about his project; the following pages, in fact, suggest otherwise. It is rather to say that the project should be taken seriously and can provide a useful input into the socialist movement.[1] Response on the left to Habermas's work has frequently taken the form either of unreserved enthusiasm or of absolute rejection, with the justification of either position never getting much beyond the level of polemics.[2] In such cases the proponents tend to label every critic a "positivist" or a victim of "objectivism," while the opponents see nothing in Habermas but "liberalism" and "idealism." But neither of these stances is likely to be very fruitful. Now more than ever is it important to avoid a sectarianism where individuals find comfort in a self-insulated theoretical tradition, but only at the cost of irrelevance. What is needed is a reasoned reception and criticism of Habermas's work within the socialist movement. My principal purpose in the following study is to promote and contribute to such a project.

The book falls rather neatly into two parts. Chapters 2-4 concern themselves primarily with a concise explication of Habermas's positive social theory and of the criticisms of Marxism which partly grow out of and partly issue in that theory. The idea here is to present as strong a case as possible for the proposed reconstruction of Marxism, in order to promote a productive discussion of the really important issues involved. The remaining chapters then take up the task of evaluating the criticisms of Marxism.

These criticisms fall into two categories. On the one hand, Habermas wants to point out certain inadequacies in Marx's critique of political economy, considered as a theory of present-day capitalism. Because of state intervention in the economy, political and economic phenomena are no longer related to each other as "superstructure" to "base." Since Marx's value-theoretical conception of capital development presupposes such a relationship, it is no longer capable of capturing the essential features of capitalist society. To comprehend certain fundamentally new developmental possibilities and tendencies in the society, a new approach is needed. On the other hand, Habermas claims, the adoption of an adequate theoretical stance is hindered by certain misformulations of historical materialism. To expose these errors is the goal of the latter group of criticisms. It is Habermas's view that there are two forms of historical progress—technical rationalization and practical rationalization—which are logically independent of each other. The first has to do with society's power of control over natural processes; the second with the justifiability of norms governing human interaction. Habermas claims that in characterizing the process of societal reproduction as production, Marx mistakenly attempts to reduce practical rationalization to technical rationalization. Habermas maintains further that this categorical framework is inappropriate for Marx's critique of political economy, which implicitly recognizes the logical independence of these two forms of progress.

In Chapter 6 I argue that these criticisms of Marx's historical materialism rest on certain misinterpretations. Roughly put, the position defended is the following: There is no clash between Marx's historical materialism and his critique of political economy. Marx consistently makes use of a conception of progress which is not captured by Habermas's notion of technical rationalization, but which does not treat technical and practical rationalization as logically independent either. Rather, the view is that these two developmental patterns are inextricably intertwined. More important, however, than whether Habermas has misread Marx is the question of an adequate conceptualization of societal reproduction, where "adequate" means roughly "appropriate for coming to grips with presen-day social reality." This question is also addressed in Chapter 6. I argue there that Marx's conceptualization is more appropriate for understanding the social role of technology—an issue which has been of central concern to the theoreticians of the Frankfurt School and which is certainly of crucial importance today. If my arguments are sound, then there are certain ways in which power relations get anchored and realized in specific modifications of the production process, and Habermas's conceptualiza-tion is inadequate to deal with these processes and the ideological mystifi-cations that arise out of them. I also argue against Habermas's claim that the productive forces are not fettered in advanced capitalism. Habermas holds this position, I believe, because his conception of technical rationali-zation yields an incorrect account of what development of the productive forces amounts to.

In Chapter 5 I lay a partial basis for the aforementioned arguments by presenting an interpretation of Marx's critique of political economy. This interpretation tries to clarify certain features of Marx's theory which are quite difficult to understand and which indeed have frequently been misunderstood, even within the socialist movement. In particular I try to make clear the sense in which value and capital are for Marx necessarily reified expressions of social relations of production. My hope is that this chapter will have independent value as an introduction to Marx's theory of capitalism and that it may serve as a useful aid in the study of *Capital*.

Chapter 7 deals with the most important of Habermas's criticisms of the value-theoretical conception of capitalism, namely his claim that because of the institutionalization of scientific and technological growth, the law of the tendency of the rate of profit to fall no longer holds. While a study of Marx's writings reveal that he conceived the law in such a way that, if it were true for the capitalism of his day, it could not be rendered false in the manner Habermas suggests, an evaluation of Habermas's charge cannot rest with exegesis of Marx. Once again, the primary issue is not that of a correct interpretation of Marx; it is rather, in this case, that of a correct account of the dynamics of the profit rate. And Marx's argumenta-tion is not sufficient to warrant belief in the law. The important question thus becomes whether adequate arguments can be constructed. A defini-tive answer to this question is not reached, but some important considera-tions are brought to light. Probably the main contribution of this chapter to the long-standing discussion of the law is a clarification of the relations between various sorts of technical change and what is usually called the organic composition of capital.

In Chapter 8 I try to draw out some implications of the preceding analysis and to discuss briefly some unresolved issues. I take a general position with regard to Habermas's claim that Marx's value-theoretical analysis of capitalism is no longer adequate. One must concede, I think, that it is quite important for coming to grips with modern capitalism to adopt a research strategy which investigates the possibility of crisis due, in some sense, to a nonoptimal environment for capital. I am thinking here, for example, both of exhaustion of natural resources and of increasing demands on the state apparatus to meet needs whose satisfaction (or lack thereof) was formerly left to the autonomous workings of the market. The historical development of capitalism has made such investigations more important now than they were in Marx's day, and the pursuance of them is perhaps the most promising aspect of Habermas's work. On the other hand, it seems incorrect to claim, as Habermas does on some occasions, that the critique of political economy is conceptually incompatible with such a research strategy. It is still quite important to investigate a central question of Marx's project, namely whether capital has an immanent barrier, i.e., whether it is a system of social relations which must eventually break down regardless of external conditions.

There are other ways of making use of this book besides the obvious one of reading it straight through in its entirety. I have already mentioned Chapter 5 in this regard. Readers less acquainted with Marx's writing might read this chapter first. Chapter 7 could also be read independently of the rest by those who have been following the debate over Marx's theory of the profit rate. Unfortunately, some of the argumentation here presupposes some familiarity with input-output models and the associated mathematics, though I have tried always to state clearly, apart from this apparatus, *what* is being argued. Those readers interested primarily in Habermas's criticisms of the value-theoretical conception of capitalism might wish to restrict themselves to Chapter 3, pp. 55-68 and Chapters, 5, 7, and 8, while those interested primarily in the critique of Marx's historical materialism might read only Chapters 2, 3, pp. 68-75 and Chapters 5, 6, and 8.

NOTES

1. Habermas's own political commitment is evident from his recent forthright stand in defense of the left in Germany against increasingly repressive measures, often taken against leftist intellectuals under the pretext that in virtue of their critical views

they are responsible for terrorism. See his "Stumpf gewordene Waffen aus dem Arsenal der Gegenaufklärung," in *Briefe zur Verteidigung der Republic,* ed. by Freimut Duve, Heinrich Böll, and Klaus Staeck (Reinbek bei Hamburg: Rowohlt Taschenbuch Verlag, 1977), and "A test for popular justice: the accusations against the intellectuals," trans. from *Der Spiegel* (October 10, 1977) by Mark Franke in *New German Critique* 12 (Fall 1977): 11-13.

2. In my opinion this is *not* true of Tony Flood, "Jürgen Habermas's critique of Marxism," *Science and Society* XLI (Winter 1977-78): 448-64. While more sympathetic to Habermas's critique than the present study, Flood's essay makes a serious attempt at clarification of Habermas's position and treats Habermas's view of Marxism as "a sympathetically critical one from which Marxists should learn, even as they attempt to answer it" (p. 448). Habermas's work is also considered in an open-minded way by Kai Nielson, "The political relevance of Habermas," *Radical Philosophers Newsjournal* VII (August 1976): 1-11.

Chapter 2

THE EPISTEMOLOGY OF CRITICAL THEORY

Habermas's work comes out of a tradition concerned with developing a "critical theory of society," especially as this notion was formulated in the 1930s by certain members of the *Institut für Sozialforschung* (the so-called "Frankfurt School").[1] According to this tradition, an adequate social theory must be an objective, empirically falsifiable theory of social institutions, which is at the same time critical of them, aiming at their transformation into a rational social order. Such a theory, it is claimed, must have a distinctive epistemological status, which Habermas has been at great pains to formulate precisely. To explicate his conception is the goal of this chapter. In Chapter 3 we shall discuss some fundamental features of his theory of social evolution. The material in these two chapters, though to a certain extent it grows out of his critique of Marxism, is nevertheless important for an understanding of that critique. We shall explicitly take up his criticisms of Marxism in Chapter 4.

Hermeneutic and Empirical-Analytic Approaches in Social Theory

In the *Nicomachean Ethics* Aristotle distinguishes two components of the rational part of the soul: the "calculative" and the "scientific." The former is concerned with things which do, the latter with things which do not "admit of being other than they are."[2] Employment of the scientific component consists in making deductions from intuitively grasped first principles.[3] This process yields *scientific knowledge (episteme),* which since its subject matter is invariable, consists of universal and necessary truths.[4] In contrast, the calculative component is employed in calculation or deliberation concerning the attainment of certain ends in human activity. As we shall see, this process yields something less than universal and necessary truths. It yields either *productive knowledge* or *practical knowledge,* depending on whether the activity in question is production (*poiesis*) or action (*praxis*).[5] Both production (making things) and action (doing things) are concerned with achieving certain ends. But production aims at an end outside of itself (viz. the product) while action does not; for "good action is itself an end."[6] Production is activity performed for the sake of something else, while action is performed for its own sake.

Habermas makes a distinction, which he traces back to the Aristotelian one between *poiesis* and *praxis,* between *purposive-rational action* (*zweckrationales Handeln*) and *communicative action* (*kommunikatives Handeln*) on the other. This distinction is quite central to his social-theoretical endeavors. Purposive-rational action consists of instrumental action, strategic action, or their conjunction. Instrumental action is the *utilization* of means to achieve given ends; it is guided by technical rules, which are based on empirical knowledge. Strategic action is the *selection* of appropriate means to achieve given ends; it is guided by strategies, which are obtained by way of deduction from preference structures and decision principles. In purposive-rational action, the agent adopts preferences and decision principles "monologically," i.e., independently of consensus with other agents. Communicative action, on the other hand, is a symbolically mediated interaction which proceeds "dialogically," i.e., on the basis of intersubjectively binding norms; these norms "define reciprocal expectations about behavior and must be understood and acknowledged by at least two acting subjects."[7] This definition of *praxis* as *interaction* which is *symbolically mediated* stresses its social and communicative character, a feature which is missing from Aristotle's *definition,* though to be sure he considered good action possible only within and through the pedagogical mediation of society. The significance of this feature will be discussed shortly.

The difference between purposive-rational action and communicative action is further revealed in the consequences of failure in the two spheres:

Incompetent behavior, which violates valid technical rules or strategies, is condemned by lack of success *per se*; the "punishment" is so to speak built into the rebuff by reality. *Deviant* behavior, which violates consensual norms, provokes sanctions that are connected with the rules only externally, that is by convention.[8]

Similarly, the sorts of problems encountered in each sphere are different:

Technical questions are posed with a view to the rationally goal-directed organization of means and rational choice among alternative means, once the goals (values and maxims) are given. Practical questions, on the other hand, are posed with a view to the acceptance or rejection of norms, especially norms for action, the claims to validity of which we can support or oppose with reasons.[9]

For Aristotle, the capacity to deal rationally with technical problems is different in kind from the capacity to deal rationally with practical problems: "Production is different from action. . . . Hence the characteristic of acting rationally is different from the characteristic of producing rationally."[10] Productive or technical knowledge is art or skill (*techne*), while practical knowledge is prudence (*phronesis*), which is a capacity for rational deliberation concerning not what sorts of things are good for the sake of something else but rather what is good for its own sake, viz. good action, the good life (*eupraxia*).[11] And although politics makes use of technical knowledge, it is basically a branch of practical knowledge, since it concerns "an end in the realm of action which we desire for its own sake, an end which determines all our other desires," viz. "the good for man."[12]

It is Habermas's view that modern social science has lost this orientation toward practical questions; what remains is an exclusively technical perspective. This development began as early as Machiavelli:

Machiavelli reduces the practical knowledge of politics to a technical skill. For the Ancients, too, the politicians entrusted with the direction of the state were to combine their prudence with certain capabilities, say, the mastery of economics or of military strategy. With Machiavelli, however, only the artisanlike skill of the strategist remains for politics.[13]

There is a further difference between the new and the old politics, however—one not yet present with Machiavelli: its scientific pretensions.

For Aristotle, since practical affairs "admit of being other than they are," politics cannot claim the apodictic epistemic status of scientific knowledge.[14] The latter is part of *theoria,* which is disinterested contemplation of an ontologically fixed cosmos. There is no room here for the calculation or deliberation required in practical affairs; only demonstration from intuitively apprehended first principles is appropriate. Conversely, the inconstancy of practical affairs and their relativity to human purpose preclude any demonstration which could ground politics theoretically. In this sense the spheres of theory and practice are incommensurable, though to be sure they are both subject to the power of *logos* and thus admit of rational treatment.

According to Habermas, a signal feature of the scientific revolution is the transformation of science into knowledge which, though theoretical, is applicable in principle. Because of its fusion with an experimental approach, theory gains access to the realm of human activity. With this development, the demand for a science of society, a scientific politics, could be raised. The new applicability of theory, however, is one-sided. It is limited to the treatment of technical questions, to the realm of *poiesis; praxis* is still excluded. For this reason, when Hobbes attempts to put social philosophy on a scientific basis, he reinforces and secures methodologically the technical perspective initiated but only treated pragmatically by Machiavelli.[15] While Habermas rejects this Galilean paradigm for social science because it cannot deal with practical questions, he nevertheless wants to retain the goal of constructing a social theory which has a scientific status. Before we can characterize in detail this attempted synthesis of Aristotelian and Galilean approaches, some additional groundwork is necessary.

For Habermas, the reason why the scientific revolution created for theory access only to *poiesis* and not to *praxis* is that its product, empirical-analytic science, is basically the pursuit of theory "with the attitude of the technician."[16] He is quick to point out that this "attitude" is not (necessarily) a subjective intention on the part of the working scientist.[17] It is rather an "interest" which is objectively rooted in the "logic of inquiry" itself. It is "knowledge-constitutive" in that it has the transcendental function of determining the basic features of the object domain of the theory and the sort of application to which the theory is amenable. It does not mar the objectivity of the theory; rather it determines "the aspect under which reality is objectified and can thus be made accessible to experience to begin with."[18]

As we shall see in the next chapter, Habermas sees specifically human development beginning when humans distinguish themselves from other hominids by reproducing their life through social labor processes, which are embedded in a specific kind of family structure.[19] At this stage both technical and practical questions come into being along with anthropologically deep-rooted interests in their solution.[20] These interests are the two most fundamental knowledge-constitutive interests, the *technical* and the *practical* interests of knowledge. The former is the interest in technical control which is implicit in the behavioral sphere of purposive-rational action. The latter aims at the attainment of action-orienting mutual understanding among individuals who interact with each other symbolically. This interest is inherent in the structure of symbolic interaction, and it serves the formation of ego and group identities, which determine mutual expectations about behavior.

Each of the cognitive interests guides the development of a corresponding type of science. The technical interest guides the development of the *empirical-analytic* sciences, while the practical interest is constitutive of the *hermeneutic* disciplines.[21] This two-fold classification of forms of inquiry is a modified form of Dilthey's classification of the sciences into the natural sciences (*Naturwissenschaften*) and the cultural sciences (*Geisteswissenschaften*).[22] Habermas's distinction is made epistemologically rather than on the basis of differences in subject matter (so that one can speak of an empirical-analytic *social* science, for example). In formulating his classification, however, Habermas appeals to the distinction first worked out systematically by Dilthey between explanation (*Erklären*) and understanding (*Verstehen*).[23] Empirical-analytic sciences aim at the former; the hermeneutic sciences, at the latter. Empirical-analytic theories are hypothetical-deductive systems of propositions constructed so as to yield deductive-nomological explanations of observable phenomena. Classical mechanics is an example of an empirical-analytic theory. The hermeneutical sciences, on the other hand, are not constructed deductively; on the contrary, they are in principle unformalizable, because they make use of the reflexivity of ordinary language in order to achieve understanding of meanings expressed in ordinary language.[24] The aim is to secure interpretations of cultural tradition; the method used is hermeneutics, which makes use of a process of feedback correction between a preliminary global understanding of a text to be interpreted and interpretations of its parts. Philology is an example of a hermeneutic discipline.[25]

These two types of science depend on their respective constitutive interests in two areas, as stated earlier: the formation of the object domain of the theory, and the conditions of the theory's possible application. The first connection is explained by Habermas as follows:

In the functional sphere of instrumental action we encounter objects of the type of moving bodies; here we experience things, events, and conditions which are, in principle, capable of being manipulated. In interactions (or at the level of possible intersubjective communication) we encounter objects of the type of speaking and acting subjects; here we experience persons, utterances and conditions which are in principle symbolically structured and understandable. The object domains of the empirical-analytic and of the hermeneutic sciences are based on these objectifications of reality, which we undertake daily always from the viewpoint either of technical control or intersubjective communication. This is revealed by a methodological comparison of the fundamental theoretical concepts, the logical construction of theorems, the relationship of theory to the object domain, the criteria of verification, the testing procedures, and so forth.[26]

In the behavioral sphere of purposive-rational action, we conceptualize reality in such a way that the objects we encounter are in principle capable of being manipulated. That is to say, the categories under which reality is disclosed to us in the sphere of purposive-rational action are determined by the interest in technical control which is implicit in that activity. In empirical-analytic inquiry, data are acquired through systematic observation, which has the form of an experimental or quasi-experimental undertaking. This process has structural (logical) similarities to purposive-rational action; in fact, it is a systematic continuation of the learning process occurring on a prescientific level within that behavioral sphere. These similarities guarantee that the object domains of empirical-analytic science are structured by the technical cognitive interest. And similarly for hermeneutical inquiry: these sciences lend methodical form to the process of arriving at mutual understanding which takes place prescientifically in the sphere of communicative action; consequently, the object domains owe their basic structure to the practical cognitive interest.[27]

In spite of these connections with realms of human activity, the two forms of inquiry remain in a certain sense theoretical. The theory of knowledge-constitutive interests rejects the view of theory, shared by both the ancients and by modern positivism, as contemplation of an ontologically fixed cosmos, that is, of a reality which is structured independently of the knowing subject. On the other hand, the *methodological* view of the theoretical attitude as disinterested contemplation is in a certain respect preserved:

It is possible, in a sense, to conceive of the constitution of *scientific* object domains as a continuation of the objectivations that are going on in practical life. But when science seriously claims to be "objective" it bases this claim on an (institutionally guaranteed) fundamental (and not only pragmatic) decision to suspend the pressures of experience and action, thereby enabling us to test *hypothetical* truth claims through discourses and to accumulate *corroborated* knowledge or, what is the same thing, to build theories.[28]

The concept of the theoretical attitude is preserved in Habermas's concept of discourse, a form of communication differing from symbolic interaction.[29] In the latter linguistic utterances are bound together with actions and bodily expressions in established language games. Rule-guided substitutions may take place among these three classes of activities. Consequently, interactions may be completely nonverbal; however, linguistic expressions are always implied in them. A smoothly functioning interaction rests on an underlying consensus which consists in the reciprocal acknowledgement of at least four claims to validity (*Geltungsansprüche*) involved in the exchange of speech acts: that the speech act is understandable, that what it asserts is true, that its performance is right or appropriate (i.e., takes place in accordance with a correct norm) and that the speaker is authentic or sincere (*wahrhaftig*) in performing it. A refusal to recognize one or more of these claims breaks the background consensus. In such a situation specific sorts of procedures are called for to test the claims and thereby restore consensus. These procedures differ for each type of claim. *Discourse* is the special form of communication in which claims of the truth of assertions and of the correctness of norms are redeemed. Habermas calls both of these claims truth claims, because according to him, they are both capable of objective validation (or refutation) via discourse, which is a process of rational argumentation. Since truth claims of assertions have a different logic of justification from that of truth claims of norms, there is a different type of discourse appropriate to each. The truth claims of assertions are tested in *theoretical* discourse; of norms, in *practical* discourse.[30] This distinction between theoretical and practical discourse should not obscure the fact that both types of discourse are theoretical in that they require a break with the normal contexts of interaction. In contrast to interaction, only linguistic utterances form a part of discourse; "to be sure, actions and expressions of the participants accompany the discourse, but they are not components of it."[31] In discourse the only compulsion is the force of the better argument; it is guided neither by the pressures of action nor by the operation of any motives other than the desire of the participants to cooperate in a search for truth.

Critical Theory as a Synthesis of the Two Approaches

Thus the dependence of the ontological structure of reality on human interest does not for Habermas vitiate the possibility of a theoretical attitude, which may exist when the institutional prerequisites for discourse are present. It does, however, as we mentioned earlier, predetermine the specific ways in which theories can be applied:

> The opinions which form the input of discourse—and thus the raw material which is subject to argumentation with the aim of substantiation—do indeed have their origin in the diverse interrelations of experience and action. The logic of these experiential relations is manifested even in discourse itself by the fact that opinions can only be specified, and their derivation made clear, in languages of a specific form and can only be tested by methods of a specific kind (on a high level of generalization): by "observation" and "interviewing." Therefore the discursively substantiated theoretical statements (which survive argumentation) can in turn be relevant only to specific contexts of application: statements about the phenomenal domain of things and events . . . can only be translated back into orientations for purposive-rational action (in technologies and strategies); statements about the phenomenal domain of persons and utterances . . . can only be translated back into orientations for communicative action (in practical knowledge).[32]

Thus for Habermas, the dependence of empirical-analytic inquiry on the technical cognitive interest vitiates the Hobbesian ideal of a social science constructed on the model of physics. Such an attempt inevitably reduces practical questions to technical ones, since it ignores the communicative aspects of *praxis* by orienting itself exclusively toward systematic observation, which is a procedure that "brackets out" the subjectivity of the investigator. An adequate social science must reject this exclusive orientation and avail itself of the interpretive technique of hermeneutics, a procedure which goes beyond systematic observation to gain data through understanding of meanings.

> When the object domain consists of symbolically structured formations which are generated according to underlying rule systems, then the categorical framework cannot remain indifferent to that which is specific to ordinary language communication. Access to data via understanding of meanings must be permitted. From this results the problem of measurement which is typical for the social sciences. In

place of controlled observation, which guarantees the anonymity (exchangeability) of the observing subject and thus of the reproducibility of the observation, there arises a participatory relation of the understanding subject to the subject confronting him (alter ego). The paradigm is no longer the observation but the dialogue—thus a communication in which the understanding subject must invest a part of his subjectivity. . . . [In this process] we employ hermeneutics rather than a measurement procedure, which hermeneutics is not.[33]

Although Habermas therefore rejects as inadequate the Galilean paradigm for social science, he does not want simply to revert to the Aristotelian conception of politics. While he wants to achieve the access to *praxis* of the latter, he does not want to give up the scientific pretensions of the former. He formulates his problem as follows:

how can the promise of practical politics—namely, of providing practical orientation about what is right and just in a given situation—be redeemed without relinquishing the rigor of scientific knowledge, which modern social philosophy demands in contrast to the practical philosophy of classicism? And conversely, how can the promise of social philosophy to furnish a theoretical analysis of the interrelationships of social life be redeemed without relinquishing the practical orientation of classical politics?[34]

In this sense Habermas is aiming, much as Vico was, at a synthesis of the classical and modern approaches.[35]

It is clear from the foregoing that this synthesis cannot be guided solely by the technical cognitive interest. For such a theory could be applied only for purposes of technical control and thus not for the solution of practical questions. Yet, contrary perhaps to expectations, an adequate social theory cannot according to Habermas be a purely hermeneutic science, i.e., one guided only by the practical cognitive interest. In one sense practical problems are "solved" when norms for action are mutually acknowledged and internalized by members of a society. In this sense hermeneutics, which serves the reaching of such a consensus concerning norms by providing interpretations of cultural tradition which secure a sense of self for individuals and groups, can provide solutions to practical problems. Yet such "solutions" are not really solutions if the acknowledged norms are not rationally justifiable norms—if the consensus actually achieved is not a true, i.e., discursively attainable, one. The hermeneutics developed by Dilthey and others for the *Geisteswissenschaften* is inadequate, Habermas claims, precisely because it provides no safeguards against attaining a false consensus rather than a true one. In fact, this procedure, which Habermas calls "simple hermeneutic understanding" and sometimes simply "understanding of meaning" (*Sinnverstehen*), is more likely under present historical conditions to lead to a false than to a true consensus.

The reasoning here is as follows. Solutions to practical questions can only be verified in practical discourse. A prerequisite of practical discourse is that all participants are sincere or authentic (*wahrhaftig*) with respect to themselves and each other.[36] This condition is necessary to insure that the desire for a cooperative search for truth is the only motive operant in the discourse. Now the method of simple hermeneutics is geared exclusively toward achieving an understanding of *consciously expressed* intentions. Such an approach automatically assumes the sincerity of the individual with regard both to himself and to others. Thus, for example, attributions of rationalization or self-deception are not permitted in an interpretation gained through simple hermeneutics. This limitation results from the fact that the hermeneutical procedure is a methodical extension of the process of arriving at an understanding which takes place in everyday communicative interaction. All participants in an interaction must act (during the interaction) under the often contrafactual assumption that the language game is a "pure" dialog, i.e., that it conforms to the model of what Habermas calls *pure communicative action*.[37] In this ideal form of communication the participants are responsible subjects fully accountable for their actions. They are conscious of all norms which they follow, and they follow only those norms which they believe correct and for which they could offer justifications. Consequently, they act neither from unconscious motives nor on the basis of intentions to deceive. In other words we must *assume* in an interaction a condition which must be *secured* in order for practical questions to admit of rational treatment: that the participants are authentic in their actions and thus satisfy a necessary condition for practical discourse. Consequently, simple hermeneutics, which also makes this assumption, provides no safeguards against the achievement of a false consensus, one which is secured through deception and self-deception and which would not stand discursive testing.

> Thus every consensus in which the understanding of meaning terminates is in principle subject to the suspicion of being pseudo-communicatively forced: the Ancients called it delusion, when under the appearance of a factual consensus, misunderstanding and self-misunderstanding are perpetuated untouched.[38]

The hermeneutic sciences in a certain sense take the contents of cultural tradition at their face value. This is not to say that texts cannot be recognized as mutilated or distorted; it simply means that all distortions must be regarded as externally induced, i.e., as accidental from the point of view of the structure of communication itself.

[P]hilology, in its concern with symbolic structures, remains restricted to a language in which conscious intentions are expressed. By rendering objectivations [Objektivation][39] understandable, philology actualizes their intentional content in the medium of everyday life experience. To this extent philology only supplements the ability of life-historical memory as it would function under normal conditions. What it eliminates through the labor of criticism are only accidental flaws. The omissions and distortions removed by philological criticism have no systematic role. For the meaning structure of the texts studied by hermeneutics is always threatened only by the impact of external conditions. Meaning can be destroyed through the capacity and efficiency limitations of the channels of transmission, whether of memory or cultural tradition.[40]

In restricting itself methodologically to the interpretation of consciously expressed intentions, hermeneutics cannot take into account *systematic* distortions in communication, i.e., distortions due neither to faulty channels of transmission nor to accidental errors on the part of the author (such as, for example, a slip of the pen which is not an expression of some unconscious motive) but rather to systematically produced inadequacies in the semantic structure of communication itself.

This notion of systematically distorted communication may be elucidated by reference to a communication structure which excludes such distortions. This structure Habermas calls the *ideal speech situation*.[41] It is characterized formally by the symmetrical distribution of chances to assume dialogue roles, i.e., to select and employ speech acts. In particular, (1) all potential participants in discourse must have the same chance to initiate discourses and to perpetuate them through asking and answering questions, making and replying to objections, giving arguments and justifications, etc. This requirement insures that all opinions and norms are potentially subject to discursive examination. Furthermore, (2) all participants in interaction must have the same chance to express their feelings, intentions, attitudes, etc. This requirement is meant to insure the authenticity of the participants, i.e., the transparency of their inner natures to themselves and to each other. Finally, (3) all participants in interaction must have the same chance to give orders, to permit, to forbid, to give and to receive promises, etc.; in short, there must be a reciprocity in behavior expectations which excludes all privileges in the sense of one-sidedly binding norms.

The second and third requirements taken together guarantee that all symbolic interaction in the ideal speech situation is "pure" in the sense specified earlier. The first and third requirements taken together guarantee that discourse can be initiated whenever truth claims (concerning either assertions or norms) become problematic in interaction and that the discourses which are taken up are "pure" in that they are truly free from the constraints of action and reach consensus solely through the force of the better argument. As noted earlier, Habermas explicates the notion of truth by means of the idea of a rationally attained consensus.[42] The properties of the ideal speech situation spell out what it means for a consensus to be rationally attained. Since these properties place restraints on the structure of symbolic interaction as well as the structure of discourse, the idea of a rationally grounded consensus presupposes a certain type of society, a certain form of life. In fact, the three conditions of the ideal speech situation represent linguistic conceptualizations of the ideas of truth, freedom, and justice, respectively. Their interlocking shows that truth cannot be analyzed independently of freedom and justice.

Institutionally secured deviations from the ideal speech situation produce systematic distortions in communication. For example, repressive socialization processes hinder self-expression and produce neurotic disturbances. Such disturbances render certain intentions unconscious and therefore produce deviations from the model of pure communicative action. These deviations manifest themselves in certain violations of the rules of established language games, e.g., as in compulsive behavior patterns. The interrelation of utterances, actions, and expressions no longer conforms to the "grammar" of the language game. These distortions are not accidental, as in the case of a type-setting error, for example. Rather they result from the structure of communication itself; they have meaning *as distortions,* insofar as they simultaneously express and conceal unconscious intentions.[43]

Neurotic behavior patterns have objective power over their victims despite the fact that they are produced by the victims themselves. The neurotic individual does not understand his own actions, which spring from motives that, though they are his motives, have been banished from his consciousness. He has alienated a part of himself from himself and given it objective powers over him. The true meaning of his pathological behavior patterns differs from their apparent meaning, which is expressed in rationalizations. Rationalizations serve to conceal from him the true cause of his behavior; at the same time, they themselves result from and express the irrational state of affairs which is his illness. Not truly rational, rationalizations can be criticized and seen through. Psychoanalysis helps the patient to accomplish this task, by means of which he regains his rational powers and becomes the conscious author of his own actions.

Ideologies are rationalizations writ large. Instead of individual behavior patterns they serve to legitimate institutions which are not discursively justifiable. Such institutions, like neurotic behavior patterns, have objective power over individuals, in spite of the fact that they are produced by the reciprocal behavioral expectations of these individuals in their interactions with each other. These institutions express conditions which are social; they express the society's answers to practical questions and are thus in principle amenable to practical deliberation and control. That is to say, it is possible in principle for social institutions to be evaluated in discourse. Such an evaluative procedure would allow only *generalizable* interests—those interests that all persons, as fully competent subjects, would regard as legitimate—to be secured institutionally. It thereby would result in the formation of a rational general will.

> [T]he "rationality" of the discursively formed will consists in the fact that the reciprocal behavioral expectations raised to normative status afford validity to a *common* interest ascertained *without deception*. The interest is common because the constraint-free consensus permits only what *all* can want; it is free of deception because even the interpretations of needs in which *each individual* must be able to recognize what he wants become the object of discursive will-formation.[44]

The institutions of social systems characterized by systematically distorted communication, however, are out of the reach of this rational will, just as compulsive behavior patterns are not under the rational control of their victim. Rather, they operate "behind the backs" of individuals, independently of their conscious will.

> These types of social systems are in a way nature, pseudo-nature. In these systems interactions are determined in an institutional setting which is not freely accessible to the consciousness of the actors; they are acting under the violence of intentions which are not immediately their own. These are the latent intentions of social systems acting, so to say, behind the back of the individual actors.[45]

Ideologies give spurious support to the assumption of accountability—that we are conscious of and capable of discursively justifying the norms which we follow—which we must make when we participate in interaction.[46] They thus serve to prevent the demand for discursive validation of social institutions from arising by providing legitimations which conceal the nongeneralizable character of the interests furthered by these institutions. At the same time they are, like rationalizations, expressions of this irrational state of affairs. Not truly rational, they can be criticized and seen through. It is the task of an adequate social theory to further this process. Such a theory would be a *critical theory of society,* one which, through an explanation of the origin of social institutions in nongeneraliza-ble interests, simultaneously provides a critique of the ideologies that secure such institutions. Habermas sees a prime example of this type of theory in Marx's critique of political economy, viewed as a theory of the capitalist social order of his day. In providing an explanation of the operation of that society, it simultaneously exposed the pseudonatural character of its economic categories; in particular, it revealed the process of exploitation hidden under the ideological veil of the free labor contract.[47]

It is the inability to be critical of ideology that makes hermeneutics inadequate as an exclusive method for social theory. A theory that is oriented toward the solution of practical questions must regard the mem-bers of society as at least *potentially* fully accountable subjects; for this reason an exclusively empirical-analytic approach is inadequate. Yet the theory must also be cognizant of systematically distorted communications in which the members of society do not stand toward their social institu-tions as fully responsible subjects. Only to the extent that social theory can explain the origin and perpetuation of such institutions in systematic barriers to the practically rational formation of a general will (in the same way that psychoanalysis yields explanations of the origin of pathological behavior patterns in blockages of self-expression) can the members of society be enlightened as to their true condition and hence *become* fully responsible subjects. Hermeneutics cannot provide such explanations. What is needed is an understanding of distortions in communication which simultaneously explains how the distortions have arisen. As Habermas puts it with regard to psychoanalysis:

> From the viewpoint of a logic of explanation, this example of the semantic analysis of specific incomprehensible manifestations is of interest because, in a unique way, it affords simultaneous hermeneu-tic understanding and causal explanation. The analyst's understand-

ing owes its explanatory power . . . to the fact that the clarification of a systematically inaccessible meaning succeeds only to the extent to which the origin of the faulty or misleading meaning is explained. The reconstruction of the original scene [i.e., the situation in which self-expression was repressed—J.S.] makes both possible at the same time: the reconstruction leads to an understanding of the meaning of a deformed language game and simultaneously explains the origin of the deformation itself.[48]

Critical social theory must be a synthesis of the empirical-analytic and hermeneutic approaches. For its yield Habermas uses the catch-word "explanatory understanding"[49] to distinguish it from the explanation yielded by empirical-analytic science and the understanding yielded by hermeneutics.

Philosophical Foundations of Critical Theory

At the foundational level critical theory rests on a *theory of communicative competence* (or as Habermas sometimes calls it, *universal pragmatics*), which spells out the nature of the competence which an individual must possess in order to be able to "generate" or produce pure communicative situations. These situations have the structure of "pure intersubjectivity"[50]: in them both interaction and discourse are pure in the senses specified earlier, and transition to discourse from interaction is unhindered. An explication of the competence to produce such situations yields a model of undistorted communication. In this respect the theory of communicative competence brings to light the presuppositions of rational speech.

Using the model of undistorted communication as a guide, critical theory then seeks to locate and explain systematic deviations from it which have arisen under actual historical conditions. The resulting hypotheses must of course survive the test of theoretical discourse. But a further verification procedure is required which distinguishes critical theory from empirical-analytic science. This procedure is a process of enlightenment similar to the analytic conversation between doctor and patient and consequently may be called "therapeutic discourse."[51] It is a dialogue between the theorist and the addressees of the theory in which the latter come to accept the proposed hypotheses as true interpretations of their situation. This affirmation by the "objects of investigation" themselves is a necessary condition for the verification of the theory, as well as for its practical efficacy.

The theory serves primarily to enlighten its addressees about the position which they occupy in an antagonistic social system and about the interests of which they can become conscious as objectively their own in this situation. Only to the extent that organized enlightenment and counsel lead to the target-group's recognizing itself in the proferred interpretations does analytically proposed interpretation become an actual consciousness and the objectively attributed interest situation the real interest of a group capable of action.[52]

The therapeutic discourse differs in two ways from the process of discourse described earlier. First, the effective equality of opportunities required in ordinary discourse is lacking in the therapeutic discourse (at least in the beginning); in fact, it is the goal of the latter to produce such a symmetrical relation among the participants. Second, the acceptance of the proposed interpretation by the addressees of the theory confirms not only the truth of the interpretation but also their authenticity, since in such an acknowledgment they see through a self-deception. Ordinarily claims to authenticity are redeemed in the context of interaction; they are not tested in ordinary discourses.

That distinctive communication in which the distortions of the communicative structure itself can be overcome is the only one in which claims to truth can be tested "discursively" together and simultaneously with a claim to authenticity, or be rejected as unjustified.[53]

The procedure described here is one which actualizes *self-reflection,* a process in which pseudonatural constraints are critically dissolved. Put positively, it is a process of enlightenment, of the achievement of autonomy and responsibility (*Mündigkeit*). The dependence of critical theory on this process for its development insures that the acquisition of knowledge coincides with the achievement of emancipation. As Habermas puts it in one place,

In self-reflection knowledge for the sake of knowledge attains congruence with the interest in autonomy and responsibility. . . . In the power of self-reflection, knowledge and interest are one.[54]

This interest in emancipation is the knowledge-guiding interest of critical theory. It aims at the overcoming of systematic distortions in communication and consequently develops only where domination is institutionalized.[55] Thus, compared with the technical and practical cognitive interests it has a derivative status; it is less "deep-rooted" anthropologically.[56] Like the technical and practical interests, it determines object domains and contexts of application. However, critical theory bears a different relation to its cognitive interest than the other sciences do to theirs. While the latter do not incorporate into their methodological self-understanding their basis in an interest structure (and thus "confront the domain of their subject matter with an objectivistic posture"),[57] critical theory consciously guides itself by reference to the existence and fulfillment of an interest in emancipation. It therefore satisfies the demand of historical materialism

to achieve an explanation of social evolution which is so comprehensive that it even embraces both the context of origin and the context of application of the theory itself. The theory specifies the conditions under which reflection on the history of our species by members of this species themselves has become objectively possible; and at the same time it names those to whom this theory is addressed, who can with its aid gain enlightenment about themselves and their potentially emancipatory role in the historical process. By means of the reflection on its context of origin and the anticipation of its context of application the theory comprehends itself as a necessary catalytic moment within the same complex of social life which it analyzes, and it analyzes this complex as an integral complex of constraint or compulsion [Zwangszusammenhang] from the point of view of its possible abolition [Aufhebung].[58]

At this point one might wonder how any sort of objectivity can be maintained for critical theory in the face of this partisan stance. Can a justifiable distinction be made between critical theory and ideology? Both critical theory and ideology are guided by interests; the difference is supposedly that the emancipatory interest guiding critical theory has a legitimacy which those guiding ideology do not—they are nongeneralizable or "particularistic." How is this difference to be argued for?

Habermas's answer is contained in his theory of communicative competence. This theory, as noted earlier, yields a model embodying the norms of rational speech, namely, the model of the ideal speech situation. This model depicts that form of life in which systematic distortions in communication are ruled out. Since the elimination of such distortions is precisely the goal of critical theory, the emancipatory interest aims at establishing the norms of rational speech: universal autonomy and responsibility are realized only in the ideal speech situation.

Thus, according to Habermas, the partisanship of critical theory is a partisanship in favor of the norms of rational speech, so that the question of the legitimacy of the emancipatory interest reduces itself to that of the legitimacy of the norms of rational speech. But the legitimacy of those norms, Habermas claims, cannot be (reasonably) disputed, because to dispute it would require an act of communication, and every act of communication implicitly endorses these norms. For first, every act of communication endorses the values of truth and correctness:

> Whenever we assume a theoretical attitude, whenever we engage in a discourse—indeed whenever we engage in communication at all, we thereby at least implicitly make certain presuppositions: namely, that true propositions are preferable to false propositions and that correct (i.e., justifiable) norms are preferable to incorrect ones.[59]

And second, since truth and correctness (or simply "truth," broadly conceived) are secured only in the ideal speech situation, every act of communication is an endorsement of the ideal speech situation:

> No matter how the intersubjectivity of mutual understanding may be deformed, the *design* of an ideal speech situation is necessarily implied in the structure of potential speech, since all speech, even of intentional deception, is oriented toward the idea of truth.[60]

The transcendental nature of this approach should be apparent. It is reminiscent of Aristotle's attempt in the *Metaphysics* to provide a "negative demonstration" or a "proof *ad hominem*" of the principle of contradiction. The strategy of such an attempt is to get the opponent to admit the principle in his very attempt to deny it, so that "while disowning reason he listens to reason." Aristotle is convinced that this strategy will always work because all meaningful speech presupposes the principle.[61] Similarly, Habermas would say that every act of communication, even one directed at rejecting the norms of rational speech, implicitly acknowledges these norms. The approach is also similar to Kant's transcendental justifications of the categories of the understanding. For example, the truth of the principle of universal causality is argued for as a necessary condition for empirical knowledge in general.[62] If this argument is valid, then Hume's skeptical position concerning the idea of necessary connection is untenable to the extent that formulating it requires admitting the possibility of any sort of empirical knowledge.

Habermas is not unaware of these similarities. In fact, he and his colleague Karl-Otto Apel have been explicitly concerned about formulating a theory of communication within the tradition of transcendental philosophy.[63] According to Habermas, the theory of communicative competence has the status of a "rational reconstruction," a type of knowledge which, following Chomsky's generative grammar as a paradigm, he defines as follows:

> Rational reconstructions... deal with anonymous rule systems, which any subjects whatsoever can comply with, insofar as they have acquired the corresponding competence with respect to these rules .... A successful reconstruction... raises an "unconsciously" functioning rule system to consciousness in a certain manner; it renders explicit the intuitive knowledge that is given with respect to the rules in the form of "know how."[64]

Rational reconstructions are the current heirs of transcendental philosophy:

> [T]he paradigm of language has led to a reframing of the transcendental model in a way which makes it unnecessary to add a transcendental subject to the system of conditions, categories or rules established by the theory of language... it suffices to grasp the generative nature of rules themselves, whereas the mastery of these rules, i.e., the emergence of competence and hence the formation of a competent subject, becomes a second, analytically and empirically independent, issue.[65]

This type of science includes logic, metamathematics, epistemology, and linguistics; it thus "forms the core of the philosophic disciplines." It proceeds by means of "reflection about presuppositions on which we always rely naively in rational speech."[66] This procedure gives reconstruction the status of "pure" knowledge and thus yields an a priori justification of the emancipatory interest:

> The human interest in autonomy and responsibility is not mere fancy, for it can be apprehended *a priori*. What raises us out of nature is the only thing whose nature we can know: *language*. Through its structure, autonomy and responsibility are posited for us. Our first sentence expresses unequivocally the intention of a universal and unconstrained consensus.[67]

NOTES

1. Much of the work of the Institut was published in its journal, *Zeitschrift für Sozialforschung* I-VIII (1932-1939). For English translations of some of this early work on critical theory see Herbert Marcuse, *Negations: Essays in Critical Theory*, trans. by Jeremy J. Shapiro (Boston: Beacon Press, 1968), and Max Horkheimer, *Critical Theory*, trans. by Matthew J. O'Connell et al. (New York: Herder and Herder, 1972). For an intellectual history of the Frankfurt School during the period 1923-1950, see Martin Jay, *The Dialectical Imagination* (Boston: Little, Brown, 1973). Other work on the history of the Frankfurt School, somewhat critical of Jay's interpretation, has been done by Douglas Kellner, "The Frankfurt School revisited: a critique of Martin Jay's *The Dialectical Imagination*," *New German Critique* IV (1975), and Phil Slater, *Origin and Significance of the Frankfurt School* (London: Routledge and Kegan Paul, 1977).

2. *Nicomachean Ethics*, Bk. VI, Ch. 1. I have relied on the English translations of Aristotle cited in the bibliography.

3. Ibid., Bk. VI, Chs. 3, 6, 7. *Posterior Analytics*, Bk. I, Chs. 2-3; Bk. II, Ch. 19.

4. *Posterior Analytics*, Bk. I, Ch. 4. *Nicomachean Ethics*, Bk. VI, Chs. 4, 6.

5. *Nicomachean Ethics*, Bk. VI, Chs. 2, 4, 5.

6. Ibid., Ch. 5.

7. Jürgen Habermas, "Technology and science as 'ideology,'" in *Toward A Rational Society*, trans. by Jeremy J. Shapiro (Boston: Beacon Press, 1970), pp. 91-2. Sometimes Habermas refers to communicative action simply as "interaction" and to an instance of it as "an interaction." We shall follow him in this usage. Although in much of his work Habermas seems to use "symbolically mediated interaction" and "communicative action" interchangeably—and in this study we shall not make any distinction—he has recently acknowledged a new category, that of "symbolic action," which differs from communicative action ("Was heisst Universalpragmatik?" in *Sprachpragmatik und Philosophie*, ed. by Karl-Otto Apel (Frankfurt: Suhrkamp Verlag, 1976), pp. 223-4). He seems to recognize four basic types of action: instrumental, strategic, symbolic, and communicative. As we shall see below, communicative action takes place in a context in which participants implicitly claim and reciprocally acknowledge that expressions are understandable, that their propositional content is true, that they are made in accordance with a justifiable norm, and that they are made with authenticity or sincerity (*Wahrhaftigkeit*). Symbolic action, in the new sense, differs from communicative action in not involving any claim to truth; an example would be a dance or concert. And, incidentally, strategic action differs from communicative action in not involving any claim to authenticity. This sort of action, according to Habermas, takes place in competitive situations, such as games of chess, war, and various economic contexts.

8. Ibid.

9. Habermas, *Theory and Practice*, trans. by John Viertel (Boston: Beacon Press, 1973), p. 3.

10. *Nicomachean Ethics*, Bk. VI, Ch. 4.

11. Ibid, Chs. 4-5.

12. Ibid., Bk. I, Ch. 2.

13. *Theory and Practice*, p. 59.

14. *Nicomachean Ethics*, Bk. I, Ch. 3; Bk. VI, Ch. 5.

15. *Theory and Practice*, pp. 56-8.

16. Ibid., p. 61.

17. Ibid. See also "Habermas talking: an interview," *Theory and Society* I (1974): 45.

18. *Theory and Practice*, p. 9.

19. Habermas, "Towards a reconstruction of historical materialism," *Theory and Society* II (1975): 288-9. For an expanded version of this last essay, see Habermas' book, *Zur Rekonstruktion des Historischen Materialismus* (Frankfurt: Suhrkamp, 1976), pp. 144-99.

20. Habermas, *Knowledge and Human Interests*, trans. by Jeremy J. Shapiro (Boston: Beacon Press, 1971), pp. 196-7.

21. "Knowledge and human interests: a general perspective," Appendix to *Knowledge and Human Interests*, pp. 308-10.

22. See the passage from Dilthey quoted in *Knowledge and Human Interests*, p. 141. For a history of the distinction between the two types of science, see Habermas, *Zur Logik der Sozialwissenschaften* (Frankfurt: Suhrkamp, 1970).

23. For a brief history of this distinction, see G.H. von Wright, *Explanation and Understanding* (Ithaca, N.Y.: Cornell University Press, 1971). A useful collection of readings on the concept of understanding in social theory is *Understanding and Social Inquiry*, ed. by Fred R. Dallmayr and Thomas A. McCarthy (Notre Dame and London: University of Notre Dame Press, 1977). The book also contains a useful bibliography.

24. Habermas, *Knowledge and Human Interests*, Ch. 8, and "Der Universalitatsanspruch der Hermeneutik," in Karl-Otto Apel et al., *Hermeneutik und Ideologiekritik* (Frankfurt: Suhrkamp, 1971), pp. 121-2.

25. A useful exposition of the hermeneutic approach is given by R. Palmer, *Hermeneutics* (Evanston, Ill.: Northwestern University Press, 1968). Cf., Gerard Radnitzky, *Contemporary Schools of Metascience* (Chicago: Henry Regnery, 1973), Vol. II. See also the symposium on "Hermeneutics and critical theory," in *Cultural Hermeneutics* II (February 1975): 307-90.

26. *Theory and Practice*, p. 8.

27. *Knowledge and Human Interests*, pp. 191-2.

28. Habermas, "A postscript to *Knowledge and Human Interests*," *Philosophy of the Social Sciences* III (1973): 174.

29. Thus, "discourse" is a technical term for Habermas, having a narrower meaning than, say, "conversation." The distinction between discourse and interaction is explicated by Habermas in the following places: "Vorbereitende Bemerkungen zu einer Theorie der kommunikativen Kompetenz," in Habermas and Niklas Luhmann, *Theorie der Gesellschaft oder Sozialtechnologie—Was leistet die Systemforschung?* (Frankfurt: Suhrkamp, 1971), pp. 114-22; Habermas, "Wahrheitstheorien," in *Wirklichkeit und Reflexion: Walter Schulz zum 60. Geburtstag*, ed. by Halmut Fahrenbach (Pfullingen: Verlag Gunther Neske, 1973); "A postscript to *Knowledge and Human Interests*," pp. 168ff.; and *Theory and Practice*, pp. 16-9.

30. Thus while Habermas is definitely an ethical cognitivist, he is not an ethical naturalist. He recognizes a logical difference between declarative statements and normative statements and is quite concerned to avoid the so-called naturalistic fallacy. Habermas has often been described as attempting to overcome the Humean dualism between "is" and "ought." This can be quite misleading, for according to Habermas, "Since Hume the dualism between is and ought, between facts and values, has been thoroughly clarified. It signifies the impossibility of logically deriving

38   HABERMAS AND MARXISM

prescriptive sentences or value judgments from descriptive sentences or statements"
(Habermas, *Legitimation Crisis*, trans. by Thomas McCarthy (Boston, Beacon Press,
1975), p. 102). See also "A postscript to *Knowledge and Human Interests*," p. 178
and "Wahrheitstheorien," pp. 226, 230.
    31. "Vorbereitende Bemerkungen," p. 115.
    32. *Theory and Practice*, p. 20.
    33. Ibid., pp. 10-11.
    34. Ibid., p. 44.
    35. Ibid., p. 53.
    36. "Wahrheitstheorien," p. 256.
    37. "Vorbereitende Bemerkungen," pp. 118-20.
    38. "Der Universalitätsanspruch der Hermeneutik," p. 153.
    39. The verb here is "*objectivieren*," a word which Habermas sometimes uses as
meaning to give form in a symbolic system, i.e., to make into a vehicle of communicative action. It is sometimes contrasted with "*vergegenstandlichen*," meaning to
make into an object of instrumental action. Jeremy Shapiro has rendered the former
as "objectivate" and the latter as "objectify." See his remarks on p. 323 of *Knowledge and Human Interests*. The reader should be cautioned, however, that this usage
is not consistently followed by Habermas in all his works.
    40. *Knowledge and Human Interests*, p. 216.
    41. The following explication of the concept of the ideal speech situation is
based on Habermas's discussion in the following three places: "Wahrheitstheorien,"
pp. 252-60; "Vorbereitende Bemerkungen," pp. 136-43; and Habermas, "Towards a
theory of communicative competence," *Inquiry* XIII (Winter 1970): 369-72.
    42. A helpful discussion of Habermas's theory of truth is provided by T.A.
McCarthy, "A theory of communicative competence," *Philosophy of the Social
Sciences* III (1973): 135-56.
    43. *Knowledge and Human Interests*, Ch. 10; Habermas, "On systematically
distorted communication," *Inquiry* XIII (Autumn 1970): 205-18.
    44. *Legitimation Crisis*, p. 108.
    45. "Habermas talking," p. 48.
    46. See "Vorbereitende Bemerkungen," pp. 120-21.
    47. *Knowledge and Human Interests*, pp. 59-60. We shall discuss Habermas's
interpretation of the critique of political economy in Ch. 6.
    48. "On systematically distorted communication," pp. 216-7.
    49. Ibid., p. 217; *Theory and Practice*, p. 10.
    50. "Towards a theory of communicative competence," p. 371.
    51. *Theory and Practice*, p. 23.
    52. Ibid., p. 32.
    53. Ibid., p. 24.
    54. "Knowledge and human interests: a general perspective," Appendix to
Knowledge and Human Interests, p. 314.
    55. *Theory and Practice*, p. 22.
    56. Ibid., p. 285; "Postscript," p. 176.
    57. *Theory and Practice*, p. 2.
    58. Ibid., pp. 1-2.
    59. *Zur Rekonstruktion*, p. 194.
    60. "Towards a theory of communicative competence," p. 372.
    61. *Metaphysics*, 1006a 11ff.; 1062a 5ff.

62. *Critique of Pure Reason*, trans. by Norman Kemp Smith (New York: St. Martin's, 1929) p. 219 (B 234).

63. Some of their more recent reflections on this project are contained in the volume edited by Apel, *Sprachpragmatik und Philosophie*, especially pp. 11-24, 198-204.

64. *Theory and Practice*, pp. 22-3.

65. "Postscript," p. 182.

66. *Theory and Practice*, p. 24.

67. "Knowledge and human interests: a general perspective," Appendix to *Knowledge and Human Interests*, p. 314.

Chapter 3

SOCIAL EVOLUTION

In a recent essay Habermas endorses the view that at a certain point in the process of biological evolution, hominids distinguished themselves from other primates by conferring on the reproduction of their life an economic form, i.e., a form characterized by production of tools, division of labor, and rules of product distribution. At this beginning stage of human development evolution proceeds by way of an interplay of organic and cultural mechanisms:

> On the one hand, during this period of anthropogenesis the size of the brain and important morphological features were altered on the basis of a long series of mutations. On the other hand, the environments providing selective pressures were no longer formed exclusively by the natural ecology but also by the active adaptation performances of hordes of hunting hominids.[1]

A still more advanced stage was reached, however, when this economic form of life was supplemented by a kinship structure which replaced the one-dimensional dominance hierarchy generally characteristic of verte-brates. What is specifically new about this family structure is that it is a system of social roles which is founded on the reciprocal acknowledgment of social norms; it presupposes the full development of language and marks the beginning of symbolically mediated interaction in Habermas's sense. One of these roles is the father role, with its accompanying incest taboo. At this point, Habermas suggests, we have the origin of *Homo sapiens*. The interplay between organic and cultural evolutionary mechanisms now gives way to an exclusively social evolution: Exogamy prevents the genetic isolation which could produce further speciation and also provides a basis for transmission of adaptive cultural forms. At the specifically human level, it is not species but societies which are in evolution.[2]

Habermas claims that a critical theory of contemporary capitalism must rest on a general evolutionary theory of this new phase, which he calls the *socio-cultural stage of human development.* He is currently trying to develop such a foundational theory, which he views as a "reconstruction" of historical materialism. This theory certainly has implications for the epistemology of critical theory; in fact, it includes the theory of communicative competence. So we have discussed it in part already. In this chapter, we shall discuss its more sociological and anthropological aspects. Specifically, we shall be concerned with (a) Habermas's general conceptualization of the process of social evolution, and (b) his view of historical progress.

Fundamental Concepts

The process of social evolution, Habermas claims, takes place in three dimensions: production, socialization, and system maintenance. In production, nature is appropriated by society for the satisfaction of human needs; this process takes place by means of purposive-rational action. In socialization, human beings themselves ("inner-nature") are adapted to society through communicative action. Since instrumental action is governed by technical rules (which depend on empirical knowledge) and communicative action by social norms, both production and socialization take place under the imperatives of discursively redeemable validity claims.

> Social systems adapt outer nature to society with the help of the forces of production: they organize and train labor power and develop technologies and strategies. In order to do this they require technically utilizable knowledge. . . . I see as one of the specific performances of social systems their control over outer nature through the medium of *utterances that admit of truth.* Work, or instrumental action, is governed by technical rules. The latter incor-

porate empirical assumptions that imply truth claims, that is, discursively redeemable and fundamentally criticizable claims.

Social systems adapt inner nature to society with the help of normative structures in which needs are interpreted and actions licensed or made obligatory. . . . Social systems accomplish the integration of inner nature through the medium of *norms that have need of justification.* These imply, again, a validity claim that can only be redeemed discursively.[3]

The third dimension is that of changes in a society's power of system maintenance, or, in other words, of its "steering capacity." Though Habermas rejects an exclusively systems-theoretic approach for social theory, he does make use of this originally cybernetic concept. The steering capacity of a self-regulated system is its ability to maintain itself in a "preferred" or "goal" state across internal and environmental changes. Whether or not a system is in its goal state depends on certain characteristics of the various elements of the system. These characteristics are usually called the *state variables* of the system, and a specification of values for the state variables constitutes a *state description* of the system. Certain state descriptions represent goal states of the system. Habermas calls the (vectors of) state variable values indicated in these latter descriptions the *goal values* of the system. Roughly put, the system's steering capacity increases with the range of environmental disturbances consistent with maintenance of goal values.[4]

Habermas believes that adequate conceptualizations of these three processes—production, socialization, and system maintenance—will yield three distinct "logics of development," each of which determines what counts as progress in its respective dimension. That is to say, there is a distinct concept of rationalization appropriate to each process. We might call rationalization of production *technical rationalization;* that of socialization, *practical rationalization;* and that of system maintenance, *system rationalization.*

The expressions "development," "rationalization," and "progress" are not being used here to beg any normative questions. They should be understood in this section in a way which leaves open their normative import, i.e., under what conditions they refer to changes for the better in some categorical sense. We shall address ourselves to this question in the next section, where we shall see that the normative import of system rationalization differs from that of technical and practical rationalization.

The notion of technical rationalization is Habermas's concept of growth of the forces of production. He characterizes such growth as "a socially successful implementation of knowledge with whose help we can improve the technical equipment, the organizational employment and the qualifications of existing labor power."[5] The key idea in determining levels of development for the productive forces is that of degree of potential mastery over nature, or "degree of possible disposal of natural processes."[6] The productive forces (*Produktivkräfte*) are resources for production. Their growth is measured by increases in what can be accomplished with them in production.

Practical rationalization is improvement in forms of socialization. Improvement here is to be measured "according to whether a subject in his actions authentically [*wahrhaftig*] expresses his intentions . . . and further according to whether the factually acknowledged validity claim bound up with norms of action is legitimate."[7] Both of these criteria are to be used to determine degrees of distortion of communication, which is the key idea in the developmental logic for the dimension of socialization. Rationalization here is the removal of distortions in communication.

System rationalization is of course to be defined by reference to increases in steering capacity. However, the application of the concept of steering capacity to societies runs up against problems which do not arise in the case of biological organisms. It is characteristic of a social system that its steering capacity can change either through alterations in boundaries with the environment (e.g., through exploitation of new energy sources) or through modifications in the set of goal values (as might occur, for example, if members of the society were to become satisfied with a lower standard of living). Although this is true of biological organisms to a certain extent (e.g., learning processes can increase steering capacity by adding new elements to the set of goal values, and boundary alterations such as loss of a limb can restrict steering capacity), the range of possible boundary alterations and variations of goal values consistent with the organism's identity are empirically determinable, whereas this is *not* the case with respect to social systems. In other words, Habermas views the appropriateness of the systems-theoretical framework in biology as depending on the fact that, as Ashby puts it, "the distinction between a live horse and a dead one is obvious enough."[8] What "survival" means, however, with regard to a society is by no means as empirically obvious a matter.

Organisms have clear spatial and temporal boundaries; their continued existence is characterized by goal values which vary only within empirically specifiable tolerances. Social systems, on the contrary, can assert themselves in a hypercomplex environment through altering system elements or goal values, or both, in order to maintain themselves at a new level of control. But when systems maintain themselves through altering both boundaries and structural continuity [*Bestand*], their identity becomes blurred. The same system modification can be conceived of equally well as a learning process and a change or a dissolution process and collapse of the system.[9]

Here a totally systems-theoretic approach encounters a problem it cannot handle. Its inadequacy, according to Habermas, resides in its attempt to explain phenomena of production and socialization functionally in terms of their contribution to systems maintenance. This strategy, however, requires criteria of identity enabling an identification of structures essential to the system. For the notion of steering capacity loses all usefulness apart from such criteria. Without them nothing prevents one from regarding the system's succumbing to its environment as an adoption of the latter's states as its goal state and thus as the achievement of perfect steering capacity. Furthermore, the criteria of identity cannot be regarded as rooted in the ways production and socialization are organized in the society. For if they were so regarded, then the functional explanations of developments in these spheres would be circular; e.g., a method of production is trivially system-maintaining if the identity of the system itself is defined by reference to this method. Here it becomes manifest that according to Habermas, systems theory has painted itself into a corner. Given that the clear-cut, empirical criteria of identity available for organisms is lacking in the case of social systems, the systems-theoretic approach excludes the only sources to which it could appeal for criteria of identity: principles regulating changes in production and socialization.[10]

Habermas opposes the exclusively functionalistic approach sketched above. Developments within the dimensions of social evolution cannot always be explained as functional contributions to system maintenance. Movements of a given society along the dimensions are to be explained by reference to empirical developments in conjunction with a principle, peculiar to that society, which specifies two things about that society: (1) the "learning capacity" of the society in each of the dimensions, and (2) the sorts of interdependencies which exist among changes in the three dimensions. Habermas calls this principle the society's *principle of organization (Organizationsprinzip)*. It is by reference to it that the identity problem is to be solved; for it specifies the range of possible developments which are consistent with its identity.

The formation of a society is, at any given time, determined by a fundamental principle of organization, which delimits in the abstract the possibilities for alterations of social states. By "principles of organization" I understand highly abstract regulations arising as emergent properties in improbable evolutionary steps and characterizing, at each stage, a new level of development. Organizational principles limit the capacity of a society to learn without losing its identity. According to this definition, steering problems can have crisis effects if (and only if) they cannot be resolved within the range of possibility that is circumscribed by the organizational principle of the society. Principles of organization of this type determine, firstly, the learning mechanism on which the development of the productive forces depends; they determine, secondly, the range of variation for the interpretive systems that secure identity; and finally, they fix the institutional boundaries for the possible expansion of steering capacity.[11]

It is an important consequence of this conceptualization that societies can be related to the dimensions of social evolution on two levels. The first involves locating the positions which characterize *actual* levels of functioning at a given time. The second involves circumscribing *possible* levels of functioning. A change on this level is not movement of a given type of society but rather is a change in the type of society itself.

Social evolution proceeds on two levels in that it takes place both in learning and adaptation processes at a *given* level of competence (up to the exhaustion of its structural possibilities) and also in improbable evolutionary steps which lead to new levels of competence.[12]

Thus we may speak of technical rationalization, practical rationalization and system rationalization in two senses. For example, "development of the productive forces" in its primary sense means growth in productive resources; this growth is measured by reference to the increase in productive capacity which it provides. In its secondary sense, "growth of the productive forces" means the replacement of a society with one range of possible productive capacities by another with a higher range of possible productive capacities. Similar distinctions can be made for the other two dimensions. The resolution of a given issue in social theory may turn on a disambiguation of the term "rationalization" along these lines.

Here it becomes relevant that both production and socialization are knowledge-guided processes. Production relies on rules of instrumental and strategic action, and these in turn depend on empirical and analytic knowledge. Socialization is guided by norms which have need of justification, and these norms depend on the state of practical knowledge, i.e., on society's answers to practical questions. Thus within each of these two dimensions, one type of society is more advanced than another if it allows to a greater extent the acquisition and application of the respective type of knowledge. Habermas distinguishes between nonreflexive and reflexive learning processes. The former take place "in action contexts in which implicitly raised theoretical and practical validity claims are naively taken for granted and are accepted or rejected without discursive consideration."[13] The latter take place when these validity claims are evaluated discursively. Since discourse is the proper method for evaluating such claims, reflexive learning represents an advance over nonreflexive learning.

Thus the scientific revolution was a major advance in the development of the productive forces, for it was then that the sphere of technically utilizable knowledge "was drawn into reflexive learning processes."[14] As we saw in Chapter 2, a signal feature of the scientific revolution, according to Habermas, is the transformation of science into knowledge which, though theoretical, is applicable in principle. Of course, the applicability in principle of modern science does not entail its systematic application in the productive process. Consequently, the institutional fusion of scientific and technological development, which is characteristic of twentieth-century capitalism, is also seen by Habermas as a major advance in the development of the productive forces.

In fact, for Habermas these two developments essentially complete the process of technical rationalization. Of course more productive techniques will continue to be discovered and implemented, but our learning capacity in this dimension is fully developed. Thus he makes the claim: "advanced capitalism is certainly not characterized by a fettering of the productive forces."[15]

But if our "technical reason" is in good shape, our "practical reason" is not yet fully developed. A society is handling practical questions most rationally when it guarantees that any practical issue (any issue concerning the legitimacy of norms) will be settled discursively by all those affected by the issue. In other words, practical rationalization is complete when society embodies the ideal speech situation—complete not in the sense that no better norms will ever be found or instituted but in the sense that society's learning mechanisms in the area of practical questions are fully developed. This stage has not been achieved by modern societies; there are still institutionally secured distortions in communication. Consequently "the institutionalization of general practical discourse would introduce a new stage of learning for society."[16]

I shall not present in any detail Habermas's attempts further to differentiate stages or levels of practical rationalization. For purposes of the present study it suffices to point out the approach he is using in these attempts. He leans heavily, though not uncritically, on theories of moral development in the tradition of cognitive developmental psychology. He sees a parallel between stages of development of forms of socialization and an ontogenetic logic of development of moral consciousness.[17]

While principles of organization and consequently interdependencies among developments in the three dimensions of social evolution vary from society to society, they do have some universal features. For example, there is

> a conspicuous asymmetry in the form of reproduction of socio-cultural life. While development of the productive forces always extends the scope of contingency [*Kontingenzspielraum*] of the social system, evolutionary advances in the structures of interpretive systems by no means always offer advantages of selection.[18]

Habermas is claiming that development of the productive forces works to make the environment of the system more "manageable" or less threatening, and thus would result, ceteris paribus, in an increase in steering capacity. The ceteris paribus requirement here is that no changes occur in the dimension of socialization. The analogous claim cannot be made for advances in socialization, however. As it develops, socialization becomes more and more a process of individuation. The highest stage is, as we have seen, that of socialization by means of a communicative ethic, a moral system based solely on the fundamental norms of rational speech. The establishment of such an ideal speech situation, with its guarantee against repression of self-expression, would foster maximum possible development of the individual:

> [O]n the basis of mutuality of unimpaired self-representation (which includes the acknowledgment of the self-representation of the Other as well) it is possible to achieve a significant rapport despite the inviolable distance between the partners, and that means communication under conditions of individuation.[19]

Now "socially related individuals resist, to the extent of their individuation, their incorporation without remainder into society. . . . With growing individuation the immunization of socialized individuals against decisions of the differentiated control center seem to gain in strength."[20] Consequently an advance in the mode of adaptation of inner nature to society works to diminish rather than to increase steering capacity. Thus certain state descriptions which from the nonnormative point of view of system integration could represent new goal values and consequently an increase in steering capacity may be prevented from doing so because they cannot be rendered legitimate to the increasingly individuated members of society. Certain possibilities for system integration may be inconsistent with the corresponding requirements of *social integration,* i.e., the procuring of legitimation for the institutions of the society. Consequently, the net result of an advance in the productive forces, for example, may actually be a decrease rather than an increase in steering capacity:

> We cannot exclude the possibility that a strengthening of productive forces, which heightens the power of the system, can lead to changes in normative structures that simultaneously restrict the autonomy of the system because they bring forth new legitimacy claims and thereby constrict the range of variation of the goal values.[21]

In fact, as we shall see, it is Habermas's view that such a development has occurred in contemporary capitalism. The institutionalization of scientific and technical progress has significantly strengthened the productive forces and provided an anticrisis mechanism in the economic sphere. Yet this advance has been achieved only at the cost of new forms of state activity vis-à-vis the economy, and the need for legitimation of these forms engenders new crisis tendencies.

A critical comment seems appropriate here. Habermas's claim that development of the productive forces will always increase steering capacity provided it does not precipitate destabilizing advances in socialization seems questionable on two grounds. First, a growth in productive capacity could occur without a given society's being able to utilize that capacity. This would occur if the society's economic institutions necessarily made inefficient use of some resources. Given this possibility, there is no reason to expect growth in productive forces always to enhance stability, even ceteris paribus. On the contrary, one might expect it at least sometimes to have the opposite effect. Second, there seem to be counterexamples to Habermas's claim which do not turn on the question of the possibility of resource utilization. Slave owners in the United States before the Civil War, for example, recognized that widespread literacy among slaves would endanger the institution of slavery. Surely such a development, regardless of the degree of utilization of the resulting increase in productive capacity, would have been threatening to stability entirely apart from its effects on socialization.

Historical Progress

Habermas wants his theory of social evolution to be normative as well as empirical in character. In particular, he wants to determine criteria of historical progress which he can show to be objectively justifiable. In this section we shall first consider what his standards of progress are and then how he proposes to justify them.

The reader will recall that for Habermas social evolution proceeds on two levels: that of movements of a given society along the three dimensions and that of the development of new types of society, or societies with new principles of organization. It is the latter sort of development that we are primarily concerned with here; we want to know the principles according to which Habermas proposes to make comparative evaluations of types of societies. His ideal seems to be a theory or set of principles which would yield a normatively significant one-dimensional ranking[22] of possible principles of organization, though he has not yet produced such a theory. What he is working with at present is a "two-dimensional" concept of progress: He holds technical rationalization and practical rationalization to be changes for the better. Since he holds these processes to be logically independent of each other, he is still faced with the problem of comparing two societies each of which is superior in one dimension but inferior in the other. Yet he has made some headway toward his goal, since he has identified certain types of change which in his view a theory of historical progress would have to regard as progressive.

A note of clarification: Habermas's view of advances in socialization and production as ceteris paribus progressive does not preclude his recognizing anything regressive or "bad" about them. In fact, he claims that development is often accompanied by backward steps and that this is part of the dialectical character of progress:

> Social integration which takes place through kinship relations and which is secured in cases of conflict through preconventional legal institutions belongs to a lower stage in the logic of development than social integration which occurs through relations of domination and which is secured in cases of conflict through conventional legal

institutions. In spite of this progress, the *necessary* exploitation and oppression of political class societies must, in comparison with the insignificant social inequalities which are *possible* in kinship systems, be evaluated as a backward step. Because this is so, class societies are structurally incapable of satisfying the need for legitimation which they themselves generate. Indeed, this is the key to the social dynamics of class struggle. How is this *dialectic* of progress to be explained?[23]

His answer to this question is that higher stages of development are accompanied by new needs and consequently new problems. In one respect, then, earlier stages come off better: they are not burdened with these problems. But of course, this is true only because the corresponding needs or interests are lacking. It is not that the problems are *solved* in the earlier stages; rather, they do not exist.[24] One is reminded here of Marx's remarks in the Introduction to the *Grundrisse:*

> But the difficulty lies not in understanding that the Greek arts and epic are bound up with certain forms of social development. The difficulty is that they still afford us artistic pleasure and that in a certain respect they count as a norm and as an unattainable model.
>
> A man cannot become a child again, or he becomes childish. But does he not find joy in the child's naïvete, and must he himself not strive to reproduce its truth at a higher stage? . . . Why should not the historic childhood of humanity, its most beautiful unfolding, as a stage never to return, exercise an eternal charm? The charm of [Greek] art for us is not in contradiction to the undeveloped stage of society on which it grew. [It] is its result, rather, and is inextricably bound up, rather, with the fact that the unripe social conditions under which it arose, and could alone arise, can never return.[25]

In Habermas's theory system maintenance, unlike the other two dimensions of social evolution, does not have an independent or intrinsic normative status. An increase in the steering capacity of a given society, or even an increase in the range of possible steering capacities consistent with a society's identity, is not unconditionally a development for the better, even under a ceteris paribus assumption. For such a development might mean the entrenchment of a historically backward society at the expense of a more progressive one.

Habermas's views here are tied in with his metaethical beliefs concerning how standards of progress are to be justified. Some theorists of social evolution claim that system maintenance is a good because it corresponds to, and is as well defined as survival or health in biological evolution, and the latter are seen as "objective values." This view, Habermas maintains, rests on the naturalistic fallacy:

> [T]he descriptive characterization of living systems as preferring certain states over others in no way entails a positive evaluation on the part of the observer.
>   . . . the biologist is in no way required to make into his own the tendency toward self-maintenance which he observes in living organisms—unless it is through the circumstance that he himself is a living being. However, he can abstract from this circumstance by adopting the objectivistic posture of the investigator.[26]

Matters are different, however, with respect to the values of truth and correctness. As we have seen, Habermas claims that these values receive implicit endorsement in every act of communication. Since communicative action is a form of activity fundamental to the human species, no one, no matter how objectivistic his posture, can avoid endorsing these values. But to endorse truth and correctness is to endorse the development of human beings' cognitive potential with respect to technical and practical questions, i.e., it is to endorse technical rationalization and practical rationalization. Hence progress in the dimensions of production and socialization has a normative significance which is lacking in the dimension of system maintenance:

> For organisms which maintain themselves in the structures of ordinary language communication, the validity basis [*Geltungsbasis*] of speech has the binding force of universal and unavoidable—in this sense "transcendental"—presuppositions. The *theorist* does not have the same possibility of choice with respect to the validity claims immanent in speech as he does with respect to the biologically basic value of health; for otherwise he would have to be able to dispute the very presuppositions without which the theory of evolution itself would be meaningless. . . . On these grounds I maintain that the historical-materialist criterion of progress is not arbitrary: development of the productive forces in connection with maturation of the forms of social integration represents advances in learning capacity in both dimensions—advances in objectivating knowledge and in moral-practical insight.[27]

NOTES

1. *Zur Rekonstruktion*, p. 147.

2. Ibid., pp. 145-52. Notwithstanding some puzzling remarks which Habermas makes in those pages (for example, on p. 147: "The natural evolutionary mechanism comes to a standstill"), I do not believe that he means to claim that the human gene pool is no longer changing or that such changes are not causally relevant to cultural phenomena. He means to be denying only "true speciation," i.e., the splitting of a species into several daughter species (Ernst Mayr, *Animal Species and Evolution* (Cambridge, Mass.: Harvard University Press, 1963), p. 426). It is this sort of speciation which exogamy would work against. Exogamy per se, however, would not work against "phyletic speciation"—genetic transformation without multiplication of species. However, it appears that the tremendous increase in brain size which occurred during prehuman hominid evolution created a genetic basis or potential for a phenotypic cultural evolution which proceeds much more rapidly than genetic transformation. Because of its rapidity, this process, which could well have been facilitated by exogamous kinship relations among early humans, is much more important for an understanding of social change than changes in the gene pool. There does not seem to be any justification, however, for denying the existence of the latter. On this matter see, for example, Edward O. Wilson, *Sociobiology* (Cambridge, Mass.: The Belnap Press of Harvard University Press, 1975), pp. 565-74.

3. *Legitimation Crisis*, pp. 9-10.

4. For a more detailed explication of the systems-theoretical concepts introduced in this paragraph, see Richard S. Rudner, *Philosophy of Social Science* (Englewood Cliffs, N.J.: Prentice-Hall, 1966), Ch. 5. For a rigorous formulation of a measure of degree of steering capacity, see W. Ross Ashby, *An Introduction to Cybernetics* (London: Chapman and Hall, 1956), Ch. 11.

5. *Zur Rekonstruktion*, p. 32.

6. Ibid., p. 153.

7. Ibid., p. 34.

8. W. Ross Ashby, *Design for a Brain* (London: Chapman and Hall, 1960), p. 42.

9. *Legitimation Crisis*, p. 3.

10. See Habermas's critique of Luhmann in *Theorie der Gesellschaft oder Sozialtechnologie*, especially pp. 146-70.

11. *Legitimation Crisis*, pp. 7-8.

12. *Zur Rekonstruktion*, p. 235.

13. *Legitimation Crisis*, p. 15.

14. Ibid., p. 16.

15. *Zur Rekonstruktion*, p. 53. See also "Wahrheitstheorien," p. 249, where Habermas suggests that the linking of (natural) science with discursive learning processes is "approximately" complete.

16. *Legitimation Crisis*, p. 16.

17. See, for example, *Zur Rekonstruktion*, Ch. 1.

18. *Legitimation Crisis*, p. 12.

19. "Towards a theory of communicative competence," p. 372. For a more detailed explication of socialization as a process of individuation, see the following essays by Habermas: "On social identity," *Telos* 19 (Spring 1974): 91-104; and

"Moral development and ego identity," *Telos* 24 (Summer 1975): 41-55. Ch. 3 of *Zur Rekonstruktion* is a version of the latter essay. See also Dick Howard, "Moral development and ego identity: a clarification," *Telos* 27 (Spring 1976): 176-82.

20. *Legitimation Crisis,* pp. 13-14.

21. Ibid., p. 13.

22. By "one-dimensional" ranking I simply mean an ordering—a binary relation R which is transitive and complete on its domain. Of course, if R is to be normatively significant, other constraints must be imposed. For example, the asymmetric subrelation P of R defined by

$$(x)(y) \ [Pxy \equiv Rxy \ \& \ \neg Ryx]$$

must be nonempty.

23. *Zur Rekonstruktion,* p. 180.

24. Habermas points out that this idea of development is present also in cognitive-developmental psychology (ibid., p. 45, n. 11). For example, David Elkind argues that "the transition from one form of egocentrism to another takes place in a dialectic fashion such that the mental structures which free the child from a lower form of egocentrism are the same structures which ensnare him in a higher form of egocentrism. From the developmental point of view, therefore, egocentrism can be regarded as a negative by-product of any emergent mental system in the sense that it corresponds to the fresh cognitive problems engendered by that system." "Egocentrism in adolescence," *Child Development* XXXVIII (1967): 1025.

25. Karl Marx, *Grundrisse,* trans. by Martin Nicolaus (Baltimore: Penguin, 1973), p. 111.

26. *Zur Rekonstruktion,* pp. 192, 193-4.

27. Ibid., p. 194.

Chapter 4

THE CRITIQUE OF MARXISM

For convenience of exposition, Habermas's criticisms of Marxism may be divided into two categories: those concerned with the adequacy of the critique of political economy as a theory of advanced capitalism, and those concerned with the adequacy of classical formulations of historical materialism as a categorical and epistemological framework for critical theory. On the former level, he argues that because of a new relation in modern capitalism between economic and political phenomena, Marx's value-theoretical conception of capital development no longer captures the essential features of capitalist society. The critique of political economy cannot perceive certain fundamentally new developmental possibilities and tendencies in the society; to comprehend these, a new frame of reference is needed. The adoption of an adequate theoretical stance, however, is hindered by certain misformulations of historical materialism; to expose these errors is the goal of the latter group of criticisms. Habermas claims that in several writings Marx fails to recognize socialization as a dimension of social evolution distinct from production and as a consequence formulates historical materialism in a reductionist, one-sided way. Furthermore, this misinterpretation of the historical process is accompanied by an epistemological error which is revealed in Marx's assimilation of his own work to natural science. In this chapter we shall first discuss what Habermas sees as the most important novel feature of modern capitalism and then give a brief account of the aforementioned criticisms.

Advanced Versus Liberal Capitalism

Habermas uses the term "traditional society" to refer to precapitalist civilizations, where by "civilization" is understood a class society with an organized state apparatus.[1] Traditional societies arise out of primitive social formations when a bureaucratic apparatus of authority is differentiated out of the kinship system. Production and distribution are no longer organized primarily along family lines but are rather regulated politically; the state determines a class structure by providing privileged disposition over the means of production. "The relations of production have immediately political form, i.e., economic connections are regulated by legitimate power."[2]

The principle of organization of early or "liberal" capitalism is the relation between wage labor and capital. In contrast to the class structure of traditional society, this relation is nonpolitical, since it is secured in a sphere which is free of the state, viz. the sphere of "commerce between private autonomous owners of commodities." The dominant "steering medium" (*Medium der Steuerung*) is no longer legitimate power; rather, system integration now takes place through the medium of economic exchange. Legitimate power plays a secondary role, complementary to market commerce; it is restricted to maintaining "the general conditions of production which *make possible* the market-regulated process of capital expansion [*Verwertungsprozess des Kapitals*]."[3] The actions of the state are superstructural in the sense that they do not influence the dynamic of the capital accumulation process, which develops according to its own immanent laws, but rather are mere accommodations to it. They are restricted either to *constituting* the mode of production, i.e., providing the presuppositions for the continued existence of the economy as capitalistic (e.g., by means of the system of civil law, limitation of the length of the working day, and education), or to *complementing* the market mechanism by adapting the legal system to immanently produced developments in the economy (e.g., through creating new legal arrangements in banking and business law).

The mode of legitimation or social integration in liberal capitalism also differs from that in traditional society. In the latter economic relations were justified by reference to their conformance with political authority, which, in turn, was supported by cultural tradition. In liberal capitalism the order is reversed; the political system is justified by reference to its consistency with the relations of production, which, in turn, provide their own legitimation by reference to the justice of equivalent exchange. Thus political phenomena are superstructural in a second sense: not only are they in reality mere accommodations to a self-regulated economic process, but they receive their legitimacy from this sphere as well.

In modern or advanced capitalism (*Spätkapitalismus*), however, these relationships no longer hold. The accumulation process is no longer free of politics; its own immanent development has elicited state intervention. In response to endemic crises the state has become actively engaged in the economic process. Two new sorts of governmental activity distinguish the organized capitalist state from its liberal counterpart. First, the state *replaces* the market mechanism whenever the latter leaves "functional gaps." These activities

> do not simply take into account legally economic states of affairs that have arisen independently but, *in reaction to the weaknesses of the economic driving forces,* make possible the continuance of an accumulation process no longer left to its own dynamic. Such actions thereby create new economic states of affairs.[4]

Examples of this sort of activity are Keynesian policies aimed at stimulating investment and governmental organization of activities (such as "research and development" and education) in order to heighten the productivity of labor and thereby to provide a source of new surplus value. Second, the state *compensates* for what otherwise would be politically intolerable consequences of the accumulation process by yielding to the demands of organized groups. Examples of this type of activity are repair of ecological damage and the legalization of the collective bargaining process.

A new need for legitimation is created by these additional governmental functions. The old ideology, which referred to the fairness of market exchange, is inappropriate to legitimate these new functions, since they include tampering with the market mechanism to ward off crises. The assumption by government of the role of a responsible planning authority publicly acknowledges the insufficiency of the market to achieve social justice, thereby turning what were purely economic matters into administrative ones requiring a directly political justification. Furthermore, one of the main techniques of the new categories of state activity, viz. intervention in cultural tradition (such as curriculum planning, for example), destroys the nature-like, unquestionable character of various cultural spheres by making it apparent that they could be other than they are and thereby makes all procedures or policies in these areas subject to increased pressures for legitimation:

> At every level, administrative planning produces unintended unsettling and publicizing effects. These effects weaken the justification potential of traditions that have been flushed out of their nature-like course of development. Once their unquestionable character has been destroyed, the stabilization of validity claims can succeed only through discourse. The stirring up of cultural affairs that are taken for granted thus furthers the politicization of areas of life previously assigned to the private sphere.[5]

Criticisms of Marx's Political Economy

Marx attempted to explain the crisis-ridden course of development of capitalist society in terms of its economic "laws of motion." Habermas reasons that such an attempt can succeed only if the institutional nucleus of the entire society is the economy. The economy must be an autonomous sphere, a totality which develops according to its own immanent laws. And the state must be superstructural vis-à-vis this sphere; i.e., it must provide the necessary conditions for the existence of the economy without, however, directing its development. Political and economic phenomena were related to each other in approximately this manner in liberal capitalism. However, the situation is different today, precisely (and ironically) because of developments predicted by the Marxian theory:

> The process which Marx himself prognosticated, of the concentration and centralization of capital (and correspondingly, the oligopolistic transformation of commerce), has, on the one hand, quickly and to a growing degree forced the weaker partners in the market to assert their claims in political form, and on the other hand, induced the organs of the state to intervene in the domain of commodity circulation and social labor. But in the same measure, this domain ceases to develop according to its own immanent laws. Due to the introduction of elements of the superstructure into the base itself, the classical dependency relationship of politics to the economy was disrupted.[6]

Because developments in the economy are no longer autonomous but are in part functions of governmental activity and political conflicts, the fundamental developmental tendencies and possibilities of the society cannot be captured by a theory which bases itself on the nonpolitical capital-labor relation.

Habermas has rendered this thesis more specific by stressing in his more recent work[7] three alleged inadequacies of the Marxian theory of capital development: First, governmental organization of higher education and of scientific and technological progress has provided a new source of surplus value which vitiates the law of the tendency of the rate of profit to fall as a predictor of inevitable economic crisis. Second, the institutionalization of the collective bargaining process expresses a possibly system-stabilizing class compromise which cannot be perceived from the perspective of the theory of value. And third, since the critique of political economy applied as a theory of society presupposes the superstructural character of bourgeois-democratic institutions, it cannot perceive the very real constraints which these institutions place on the procurement of legitimation for the new governmental functions of advanced capitalism; hence it fails to grasp the most likely source of crisis in this society. We now turn to an exposition of each of these charges.

REFLEXIVE LABOR AND THE RATE OF PROFIT

Although a detailed presentation of the theory that the profit rate has a tendency to fall is given in Chapter 7, a brief sketch of some of the main ideas involved is necessary here in order to make Habermas's criticisms comprehensible. The theory takes its departure from the following considerations: Associated with the process of capital accumulation are technical changes which increase the means of production employed by a given worker and thereby work to increase the total capital invested per worker. Since profit consists of surplus value, which has its origin in the surplus labor time of the workers and is not produced by the means of production employed by them, the aforementioned technical changes exert a downward pressure on the rate of profit, which is determined by the ratio of surplus value to total capital invested. Of course, this downward pressure can be counteracted somewhat by an increase in surplus labor time per worker and also by a cheapening of the means of production, but it was Marx's view that these counteracting influences could not prevent, but only retard, a fall in the rate of profit.

The following notation will allow us to spell out the theory in a little more detail:

c   value of the means of production consumed in the year's production process (annually consumed constant capital)

v   value of the capital expended for the purchase of labor power (annually consumed variable capital) s   surplus value produced during the year

r   rate of profit for the year.

Under certain simplifying assumptions[8] we may express the annual rate of profit as follows:

$$r = \frac{s}{c+v} \qquad [1]$$

Dividing both numerator and denominator by v, we get the following expression:

$$r = \frac{\frac{s}{v}}{\frac{c}{v} + 1} \qquad [2]$$

Under conditions of a constant rate of surplus value ($\frac{s}{v}$), a given variable capital v represents a definite amount of living labor; the variable capital, as Marx says, is an *index* of this amount.[9] In this case an increase in the value composition of capital ($\frac{c}{v}$) occurs exactly when the value of constant capital per worker increases.[10] Thus under these circumstances, if technical changes associated with the accumulation process bring about an increase in the value of constant capital per worker, then the concomitant rise in ($\frac{c}{v}$) will produce a fall in the rate of profit, as can easily be seen from an inspection of (2). The propensity of the accumulation process to bring about such technical changes is for Marx the source of the tendency of the profit rate to fall.

Other effects of the accumulation process, however, run counter to this downward pressure on the rate of profit. For example, productivity increases associated with capital accumulation work to lower the value of wage goods and thereby to increase the portion of the working day devoted to production of surplus value; in other words, they work to increase the rate of surplus value. Increases in the productivity of labor can also lower the value of the means of production. This cheapening of the elements of constant capital works counter to the tendency of the accumulation process to increase the value of constant capital per worker. Marx was aware of these counteracting influences; however, he claimed that the downward pressures on the rate of profit would necessarily predominate over them in the course of capital accumulation, thereby driving the economy into crisis.

Habermas focuses on this claim. He maintains that even if it was true in liberal capitalism, the conditions making it true then no longer obtain. The influence of increases in productivity in counteracting the falling tendency of the profit rate was limited in liberal capitalism because of the fortuitous nature of their source; they resulted from the utilization of inventions and information which were *externally generated* relative to the economic system.

> The institutional pressure to augment the productivity of labor through the introduction of new technology has always existed under capitalism. But innovations depended on sporadic inventions, which, while economically motivated, were still fortuitous in character.[11]

In other words, in liberal capitalism there was no systematic generation of economically utilizable, productivity-increasing innovations. It is one of the most important functions characterizing the advanced capitalist state, however, to incorporate the labor of scientists, engineers, and teachers into the economic system itself.

> Only with governmental organization of scientific-technical progress and a systematically managed expansion of the system of continuing education does the production of information, technologies, organizations, and qualifications become a component of the production process itself. Reflexive labor, that is, labor applied to itself with the aim of increasing the productivity of labor, could be regarded at first as a public good provided by nature. Today it is internalized in the economic cycle.[12]

This economic institutionalization and exploitation of scientific and technological progress places systematic emphasis on counteracting influences to the tendency of the profit rate to fall.

> Now we have capital which is invested in the area of science, technology, education, and so on, in order to boost the productivity of labor, resulting in, economically speaking, a rising rate of surplus value and in the cheapening of the constant elements of capital. This capital investment in reflexive labor is therefore a countertendency against the fall in the rate of profit already remarked about by Marx. But the difference between late capitalism and liberal capitalism, or one relevant difference is that we now incorporate these activities into the economic processes while at the time of Marx, this type of

reflexive work could be conceived of as an external input just as some natural resources such as water, etc. were.[13]

The transformation of reflexive labor from a component of the system environment into a "peculiar factor of production,"[14] renders Marx's theory of value inadequate because it provides a new form of surplus-value production not comprehended by that theory. According to Habermas, reflexive labor is not *directly* productive of surplus value, presumably because it does not produce commodities for a capitalist but rather concerns itself with developing more productive ways of producing such commodities. However, because the fruits of reflexive labor decrease the expenses of capitalist production through decreasing the value of wage commodities and the elements of constant capital, it makes it possible for the capitalist to appropriate more surplus value. Consequently Habermas, following James O'Connor,[15] calls this type of labor "indirectly productive."[16] To be sure, Marx realized these indirect effects of, for example, scientific activity. Yet for him they are not systematically produced; they have precisely the same status as the effects of weather conditions favorable to agriculture in lowering the value of wage commodities. Such a conceptual strategy is inadequate under modern conditions, where education, science, technology, and industrial utilization are fused into a system through governmental policy. This economic institutionalization of indirectly productive labor vitiates the inevitability of economic crisis asserted in the theory of the tendency of the profit rate to fall. Such crises may still occur, but they can no longer be systematically predicted; whether they occur is now a purely empirical question. The structure of the system no longer guarantees the dominance of the falling tendency of the profit rate over its counteracting tendencies.

The variable capital that is paid out as income for reflexive labor is indirectly productively invested, as it systematically alters conditions under which surplus value can be appropriated from productive labor. Thus, it indirectly contributes to production of more surplus value. This reflection shows, firstly, that the classical fundamental categories of the theory of value are insufficient for the analysis of governmental policy in education, technology, and science. It also shows that it is an empirical question whether the new form of production of surplus value can compensate for the tendential fall in the rate of profit, that is, whether it can work against economic crisis.[17]

COLLECTIVE BARGAINING AND CLASS COMPROMISE

Habermas claims that the legalized institutionalization of the collective bargaining process is a development whose significance cannot be grasped within a value-theoretical framework. For from such a perspective one must view the determination of the wage level as a purely economic process, whereas the significance of wage determination in the monopolistic sector of the economy lies in its "quasi-political" nature:

> In the monopolistic sector, by means of a coalition which has arisen between business associations and unions, the price of the commodity labor power is quasi-politically negotiated: the mechanism of competition is replaced in these "labor markets" by the formation of compromise between organizations to which the state has delegated legitimate power.[18]

Now it might seem that one could give an account of wage determination in the monopolistic sector which utilizes value-theoretical concepts. For example, just as Marx speaks of monopolies having the power to set prices above their values (more accurately: above their prices of production), one might want to say that unions have acquired the power to force the level of wages above the value of labor power. Habermas, however, claims that this route is not open to the Marxist:

> From a Marxian point of view, it is also possible, in principle, to analyze price setting in organized markets—a good can be sold above its value. But here the price of the commodity labor power is the unit of measure in the value calculation. Quasi-political price setting in the labor market cannot, therefore, be treated in an analogous way. For it determines, in turn, through the average wage level, the quantity of value against which deviations of labor power sold above value would have to be measured. We know of no standard for the costs of the reproduction of labor power which is independent of cultural norms; nor does Marx start from such a standard.[19]

Put simply: The Marxist cannot say that unions have forced wages above the value of labor power because the wage level "defines" the value of labor power. In *Capital* Marx describes the "historical and moral element" which enters into the determination of the value of labor power:

> [T]he number and extent of [the laborer's] so-called necessary wants, as also the modes of satisfying them, are themselves the

product of historical development, and depend therefore to a great extent on the degree of civilization of a country, more particularly on the conditions under which, and consequently on the habits and degree of comfort in which, the class of free laborers has been formed. In contradistinction therefore to the case of other commodities, there enters into the determination of the value of labor power a historical and moral element.[20]

Habermas claims that because the value of labor power depends in part on the culturally acceptable standard of living for a worker, it cannot be determined apart from looking at what workers actually tend to receive in return for the sale of their labor power. In this sense the average wage level is the "unit of measure in the value calculation"; that level is equal to the value of labor power "by definition." Under these conditions the idea that the wage level could be above the value of labor power, apart from temporary fluctuations, is nonsense. It is analogous to saying that the standard meter bar in Paris could be, under standard conditions, more than one meter long.

The claim is thus that the Marxist is required conceptually to equate the average wage level with the value of labor power and that such an approach is inadequate for modern capitalism because it cannot perceive the alteration in class structure inherent in the transition from an unorganized to an organized labor market. This alteration is a two-edged sword, according to Habermas. On the one hand, it has the character of a class compromise, a mitigation of the conflict between wage labor and capital, which has worked in a system-stabilizing manner. A value-theoretic perspective is blind to this development:

Of course, one can again hold fast to a dogmatic conceptual strategy and equate by definition the average wage with the costs of reproduction of labor power. But in so doing one prejudices at the analytical level the (no doubt) empirically substantial question of whether the class struggle, organized politically and through unionization, has perhaps had a stabilizing effect only because it has been successful in an economic sense and visibly altered the rate of exploitation to the advantage of the best organized parts of the working class.[21]

On the other hand, since the development of the collective bargaining process repoliticizes the relations of production, it opens the door to further alterations in class structure resulting from political conflicts which cannot themselves be explained value-theoretically.

Government activity now pursues the declared goal of steering the system so as to avoid crises, and, consequently, the class relationship has lost its unpolitical form. For these reasons, class structure *must* be maintained in struggles over the administratively mediated distribution of increases in the social product. Thus the class structure can now be directly affected by political disputes as well. Under these conditions, economic processes can no longer be conceived immanently as movements of a self-regulating economic system. . . . How, and to what extent, power is exercised and exploitation secured through economic processes depends today on concrete power constellations that are no longer *predetermined* by an autonomously effective mechanism of the labor market.[22]

Thus, Habermas claims, the classical Marxian approach is incapable of grasping both the system-maintaining and the system-endangering significance of the suspension of the liberal-capitalist unpolitical class relationship.

Habermas holds this view as a general thesis; i.e., for him it is true not only with regard to the political nature of collective bargaining but also with regard to the other new economic functions of political phenomena in advanced capitalism. We have seen how in his view the Marxian approach is inadequate to explain the system-maintaining functions of governmental policy in education, science and technology. He also holds that the repoliticization of the relations of production confers a new significance on bourgeois-democratic institutions which is not perceivable from the classical perspective. It is to this claim that we now turn.

THE LEGITIMATION CRISIS

We have seen in the beginning of this chapter that according to Habermas the reactive crisis-avoidance activities of the advanced capitalist state create legitimation problems. Tampering with the market mechanism obviously cannot be justified by appeal to the fairness of market exchange, and administrative intervention in matters formerly uncritically guided by cultural tradition raises new questions concerning the legitimacy of various arrangements and policies. A constraint on possible solutions to these problems is that the legitimate power necessary for new governmental functions must be obtained in a manner consistent with a normative system which is universalistic, since the rise of capitalism brought with it an evolutionary development of practical consciousness to the universalistic level. In particular, legitimation must be secured within the framework of political democracy based on universal suffrage.

[T]hrough the universalistic value system of bourgeois ideology, the rights of citizenship, including the right to participate in political elections, have become universal. Hence the procurement of legitimation can be disassociated from the mechanism of general elections only temporarily and under extraordinary circumstances.[23]

Political institutions democratic in form arose with liberal capitalism. They presented no threat to the existing order as long as the ideology of equivalent exchange effectively restricted political activity to securing the boundary conditions of the market economy. However, the assumption by government of the role of responsible planning authority publicly acknowledges the insufficiency of the market to achieve social justice. Consequently, in advanced capitalism the allocation of resources and the distribution of the social product become in principle matters for public deliberation. Under these circumstances the existence of formally democratic institutions presents severe problems for the continued existence of advanced capitalism. For they provide a means by which the masses of people can raise political claims for the accommodation of needs whose satisfaction was formerly the exclusive province of the market. These claims are the "demands oriented to use values,"[24] which Habermas says come into play with the growing need for legitimation of the political system. There is no guarantee that they are consistent with the requirements of capital accumulation. In fact, mass political participation would insure that they compete with those requirements, since capitalism's primary orientation is not to the generalizable interests of the population but rather to the private goals of profit maximization. Under these circumstances, the administrative system could carry out the imperatives of the economic system only by refusing to meet some of the use-value oriented demands. This strategy is viable, however, only if the refusal can be rendered acceptable to those involved. And mass political participation would foreclose this possibility.

> Genuine participation of citizens in the processes of political will-formation, that is, substantive democracy, would bring to consciousness the contradiction between administratively socialized production and the continued private appropriation and use of surplus value.[25]

The inability to render acceptable to the population at large the carrying out of the imperatives of capital accumulation is characterized by Habermas as a legitimation crisis.[26] The above argument is aimed at showing that it can be avoided only if mass loyalty is secured by means other than mass participation in the process of political decision-making. This requirement is obviously harder to satisfy under conditions of formal democracy, with its universal rights of participation, than it would be in an authoritarian system. Political abstinence cannot be enforced directly by legal means but only secured by motivational syndromes of privatism reproduced in the socio-cultural sphere. If the conditions for the reproduction of these syndromes are being eroded, as Habermas thinks they are,[27] then under the assumption that socialization continues to take place by means of norms that have need of justification, capitalism can be expected to fall into a legitimation crisis.

Thus a new level of susceptibility to crisis arises in advanced capitalism from the necessity of procuring legitimation in accordance with the procedures of formal democracy. Habermas claims that the classical Marxian conceptual strategy cannot perceive this development, since it is constrained to view the formally democratic political institutions of bourgeois society as a mere superstructure to capitalist class domination in the economic sphere and hence not a source of social crisis. This picture was adequate in liberal capitalism, when the dynamic of the economic process was nonpolitical and could justify itself by reference to the fairness of the market. In advanced capitalism, however, this dynamic is in part guided by legitimate power; the state takes on economic functions and consequently economic processes are no longer purely nonpolitical. In these circumstances the ideology of equivalent exchange is no longer viable, and economic activity must be legitimated politically. Hence the institutions of political decision-making play a new role vis-à-vis the economy and can no longer be regarded as merely superstructural.

Another way of stating Habermas's criticism is as follows: The classical conceptual strategy, since it treats the nonpolitical capital-labor relation as the institutional nucleus of the entire society, must view all social crises as problems of capital expansion. In liberal capitalism crises did indeed take the form of interruptions in the accumulation process. But aside from the fact that such system crises are no longer inevitable, the legitimation crises to which advanced capitalism is susceptible are not crises of that kind. For they can arise even when problems of capital expansion have been solved.

> Even if the state apparatus were to succeed in raising the productivity of labor and in distributing gains in productivity in such a way that an economic growth free of crises (if not disturbances) were guaranteed, growth would still be achieved in accord with priorities that take shape as a function, not of generalizable interests of the

population, but of private goals of profit maximization. The patterns of priorities that Galbraith analyzed from the point of view of "private wealth versus public poverty" result from a class structure that is, as usual, kept latent. In the final analysis, *this class structure* is the source of the legitimation deficit. . . .

The new legitimation problems cannot be subsumed under an overgeneralized imperative of self-maintenance, as they cannot be solved without regard to the satisfaction of legitimate needs—that is, to the distribution of use values—while the interests of capital accumulation prohibit precisely this consideration. Legitimation problems cannot be reduced to problems of capital expansion.[28]

Criticisms of Marx's Historical Materialism

Habermas and his colleague Albrecht Wellmer[29] have been concerned to bring to light a tension in Marx's work between his critique of political economy and the conception of history expounded in his critique of Hegelian idealism. The former satisfied the requirements for a critical theory of the capitalist society of his day. The latter, however, because it identifies historical progress with development of the forces of production, leaves no room for the sort of emancipation which results from the process of reflection elicited by critical theory. The present section is devoted to an exposition of this thesis.

We have seen (Chapter 3) that for Habermas production and socialization are two distinct dimensions of social evolution. Appropriation of outer nature takes place in the former, by means of purposive-rational action; appropriation of inner nature takes place in the latter, by means of communicative interaction. There is a distinct concept of rationalization appropriate to each of these spheres. Rationalization consists of growing theoretical-technical insight in the sphere of production and increasing practical insight in the sphere of socialization. The former is manifested in development of the productive forces; the latter, in extension of communication free of domination. These two sorts of development are logically independent of each other, and historical progress is not to be identified with either but somehow must involve both. The role of critical theory is primarily to effect progress in the sphere of socialization. By criticizing ideology it elicits a process of reflection which dissolves pseudonatural barriers to the discursive solution of practical problems.[30]

Marx's critique of political economy was aimed at providing an explanation of the operation of capitalist society which would expose the pseudonatural character of its economic institutions and the ideological nature of conceptions which took the appearance of these institutions at face value. As we shall see in Chapter 5, the analysis of the value form of commodities brought to light the specific nature of the social relations underlying commodity production, and the examination of the capital-labor relation revealed the process of exploitation which deceptively appeared as an exchange of equivalents on the market. These features of Marx's work, Habermas claims, put it squarely in the camp of critical theory. It was aimed at enlightening the proletariat concerning its objective and potentially emancipatory role in history and thereby had the immanent relation to reflection characteristic of critical theory.

However, the argument goes, in his general characterizations of the historical process Marx unwittingly rules out reflection as a motive force in history by categorizing the self-generative process of the human species as a labor process. In working out the classical formulations of historical materialism, he correctly interprets the self-formative activity of Hegel's *Geist* as a mythical expression of the developmental process of human history. However, he wrongly characterizes this process solely as a labor process; that is, he fails to recognize socialization as a dimension of social evolution distinct from production. He tries to subsume the former under the latter, to reduce interaction to labor. Social institutions and forms of consciousness thereby become for him "second-order" productive forces. Rationalization of normative systems of interaction cannot then consist in the reflective elimination of pseudonatural constraints which prevent the formation of a rational general will; rather, it can only be viewed as the replacement of institutions which are dysfunctional for the development of the productive forces (Marx speaks of "fettered" forces of production) by ones which promote this development. Practical insight is thus reduced to technical insight. In this context it is not surprising that Marx viewed his own work according to the model of natural science; for the realm of production, through the interest in technical control implicit in it, can provide only for the development of technically exploitable knowledge, the paradigm of which is, of course, natural science. Marx's theory of history entails a positivist conception of social science which is blind to the peculiar epistemological status of critique, thereby causing him to misunderstand the nature of much of his own work.

Habermas and Wellmer each cite several passages which they claim illustrate this problematic strain in Marx's work. In Habermas's original argument he claims that the line of thought was abandoned after the *Grundrisse* of 1857-1858 and that it is "typical only of the philosophical foundation of Marx's critique of Hegel, that is, production as the 'activity' of a self-constituting species."[3][1] Wellmer, however, argues that the contradiction between technocratic and ideology-critical tendencies persists into Marx's fully developed social theory and can be seen even in "specific economic analyses."[32] Both critics assert, however, that the technocratic strain is present in certain passages from the *Grundrisse* in which the transition from capitalism to socialism is anticipated. What they find problematic in these "apocryphal" passages is the role in this transition which Marx attributes to growth of the productive forces. The most important of the passages is the following:

> [T]o the degree that large industry develops, the creation of real wealth comes to depend less on labor time and on the amount of applied labor than on the power of the agencies set in motion during labor time, whose powerful effectiveness is itself in turn out of all proportion to the direct labor time spent on their production, but depends rather on the general state of science and on the progress of technology, or the application of science to production. (The development of this science, especially natural science, and all others along with it, is itself in turn related to the development of material production.) For example, agriculture becomes merely the application of the science of material metabolism as it is to be regulated most advantageously for the entire social body. Real wealth manifests itself rather—and large industry reveals this—in the tremendous disproportion between the labor time applied and its product as well as in the qualitative disproportion between labor, reduced to a pure abstraction, and the power of the production process it oversees. Labor no longer seems so much to be enclosed within the process of production, as man instead acts as the overseer and regulator of the production process. (What holds for machinery holds just as well for the combination of human activities and the development of human intercourse.) The laborer no longer inserts a modified natural object [*Naturgegenstand*] between the object [*Objekt*] and himself. Instead he inserts the process of nature, which he transforms into an industrial process, as a medium between himself and inorganic nature, which he masters. He steps to the side of the production process instead of being its chief agent. In this transformation, it is neither the direct labor which man himself performs, nor the time during which he works, but rather the appropriation of his own general productive power, his understanding of nature and his mastery over it by virtue of his presence as a social body—it is, in a word, the development of the social individual which appears as the great foundation-stone of production and of wealth. The *theft of alien labor time, on which the present wealth is based,* appears a miserable foundation in face of this new one, created by large-scale industry itself. As soon as labor in the direct form has ceased to be

the great wellspring of wealth, labor time ceases and must cease to be its measure, and hence exchange value [must cease to be the measure] of use value. *The surplus labor of the mass* has ceased to be the condition for the development of general wealth, just as the nonlabor of the few, for the development of the general powers of the human head. Therewith production based on exchange value breaks down, and the immediate material process of production is stripped of the form of penury and antagonism. The free development of individualities, and hence not the reduction of necessary labor time in order to create surplus labor, but rather the general reduction of the necessary labor of society to a minimum, which then has its counterpart in the artistic, scientific etc. development of individuals in the time set free, and with the means created, for all of them. . . .

The development of fixed capital indicates to what degree general social knowledge has become an immediate force of production, and therefore the conditions of the social life process itself have come under the control of the general intellect and have been transformed in accordance with it.[33]

Habermas interprets this passage as presenting

a model according to which the history of the species is linked to an automatic transposition of natural science and technology into a self-consciousness which controls the material life-process.[34]

And Wellmer comments as follows:

The qualitative transformation which was always conceived along with the idea of a transcendence of capitalist private ownership is now incorporated into the one-dimensional advance of a process of rationalization, at the end of which the process of social life will be organized wholly in accordance with the same principles of technical rationality which are at present largely at work in the organization of the process of production. The model taken here is not that of a practical reason that becomes actual in noncoercive communication and cooperation, but that of a technical rationality opposed to and controlling nature and society alike.[35]

What is being developed here is a theme central to the social theory of the Frankfurt School: criticism of the identification of reason with "instrumental reason."[36] Technological rationality, if developed to the extreme, would turn into a form of irrationality. The extension of this rationality to all areas of life would indeed involve liberation from material necessity. Such a development, however, would not be the fulfillment of Marx's prediction that people will come to make their history "with will and consciousness." In such a "dialectic of enlightenment," mastery over nature would be achieved at the cost of the complete subjection of the social life process—including the individuals therein—to the demands of technical control. "Accordingly, the culturally defined self-understanding of a social life-world [would be] replaced by the self-reification of men under categories of purposive-rational action and adaptive behavior."[37] The mode of socialization which consists of internalization of norms which have need of justification would be replaced by the technical manipulation of behavior. The problem of the formation of ego and group identities in such a manner that a practically rational general will comes into being would not be solved, but eliminated; in place of such a rational will would be society organized solely as a self-regulated machine-like system of purposive-rational action. In the realization of such a technocratic ideal "old regions of consciousness developed in ordinary-language communication would of necessity completely dry up ... men would make their history with will, but without consciousness."[38] Thus Marx's anticipation that the transformation of the labor process into a scientific process would automatically lead to a self-conscious control of the social life process is misguided, since it mistakenly presupposes a continuum of rationality in the treatment of technical and practical problems. Putting an end to the prehistory of human society requires, in addition to technical progress, a type of rationalization consisting of the removal of restrictions on communication:

> The course of scientific-technical progress is marked by the epochal innovations through which functional elements of the behavioral system of instrumental action are reproduced step by step at the level of machines. The limiting value of this development is thus defined: the organization of society itself as an automation. The course of the social self-formative process, on the other hand, is marked not by new technologies but by stages of reflection through which the dogmatic character of surpassed forms of domination and ideologies is dispelled, the pressure of the institutional framework is sublimated, and communicative action is set free *as* communicative action. The goal of this development is thereby anticipated: the organization of society on the exclusive basis of discussion free of domination.[39]

There are specific reasons why it is thought important to bring light and to criticize the supposed technocratic strain in Marx's thought. The failure to distinguish between technical and practical rationalization, and the resulting conception of social theory as having the epistemological status of natural science are seen as bases for errors in the socialist movement. Marx's interpretation of history, it is claimed, leads him to think that the transition to socialism can be scientifically ascertained as inevitable, independently of what the people who are thereby to achieve emancipation happen to think. Critical theory, however, must view this historical transition as *practically necessary* rather than inevitable; that is, as a transformation of society whose character and extent is dependent upon the reflective dissolution of false consciousness which occurs when the addressees of critical theory accept its interpretations as applying to their own situation. Wellmer apparently thinks Leninism and revisionism of the Bernsteinian sort are two "misconceptions" which rest on the confusion between the inevitable and the practically necessary:

[T]wo misconceptions of Marx's theory which have certain practical consequences may depend on a theoretical relationship which is more or less latent in this theory itself; I shall call them the "technocratic" and the "evolutionist" misconceptions. According to the first misconception, under certain historic initial conditions socialism would have to be brought about by an exclusive, theoretically trained, revolutionary minority ruling by authoritarian measures; according to the second, it would have to be the inevitable result of the development of capitalist society. In fact, as can easily be seen, there is only one misconception: namely, a "mechanistic" misunderstanding of historical materialism, according to which the revolution becomes the mere question of more or less expenses on the bill of history—since the end result of history is already settled.[40]

Habermas himself criticizes various conceptions of the revolutionary party for failing to distinguish between theoretical-technical and practical insight.[41] He also views this failure as at least a partial explanation for what he sees as a divergence between contemporary socialist societies and the original ideal of socialism:

Marx equates the practical insight of a political public with successful technical control. Meanwhile we have learned that even a well-functioning planning bureaucracy with scientific control of the production of goods and services is not a *sufficient* condition for realizing the associated material and intellectual productive forces in the interest of the enjoyment and freedom of an emancipated society. For Marx did not reckon with the possible emergence at every level of a discrepancy between scientific control of the material conditions of life and a democratic decision-making process. This is the philosophical reason why socialists never anticipated the authoritarian welfare state, where social wealth is relatively guaranteed while political freedom is excluded.[42]

There is another motivation for the critique of Marx we have been discussing—one which is closely tied to Habermas's endeavors to formulate a critical theory of advanced capitalist society. As we saw (pp. 65-68), Habermas's view is that a legitimation crisis can be avoided in advanced capitalism only if mass loyalty is secured without mass participation in the political decision-making process. There are ideologies which seek to justify political abstinence on the part of the masses. Among them are democratic elite theories and technocratic systems theories.[43] The former, which go back to Schumpeter and Max Weber, interpret democracy as a system in which there is a pluralism of competing elites. Mass participation is restricted to the process of selecting which elites are to have political decision-making power. It is not to be extended to the process of making the political decisions themselves, because these decisions rest on values and interests which are essentially private; no rational general agreement concerning them is possible. Science and technology may provide the ruling elites with objective information concerning the effectiveness of various means of achieving their goals; concerning the goals themselves, however, no objectivity is possible. On the other hand, the technocratic ideology, which Habermas traces back to institutionalist theories of the twenties, maintains that objectivity is possible in the treatment of social problems. These problems, however, are viewed not as practical problems but as technical ones. The technocratic ideology ironically proclaims the end of ideology; only scientific-technical knowledge, not ideological conflict, is relevant for the solution of social problems.

According to Habermas, these theories play an ideological role in modern capitalism similar to that of the classical theories of political economy in liberal capitalism. The critical theory of society must direct its efforts against them. In order to do so, however, it must both insist on the distinction between technical and practical problems and urge that the latter can receive objective treatment.[44] But it can do neither within the confines of historical materialism as classically formulated. The confusion therein of practical with technical rationalization and the consequent recognition of empirical natural science as the sole paradigm of objectively valid knowledge renders these tasks impossible. Consequently, Habermas claims, historical materialism must be reconstructed if it is to provide an adequate framework for the development of a critical theory of contemporary capitalist society. This reconstruction is to proceed, of course, along the lines indicated in Chapters 2 and 3 of the present study.

A Look Ahead

We have come to a major turning point in the discussion. The chief concern so far has been to present the strongest possible formulation of Habermas's critique of Marxism. The main focus henceforth will be appraisal of his position. Chapter 5, which presents some fundamentals of Marx's critique of political economy, lays groundwork for certain later arguments—especially in Chapter 6—which hinge on aspects of Marx's theory which in my opinion have been insufficiently understood and appreciated, even on the part of Marxists. The adequacy of Habermas's reconstruction of historical materialism, as well as the cogency of the criticisms of Marx with which it is associated, will come under examination in Chapter 6. The questions concerning the viability of Marx's political economy as a theory of advanced capitalism are taken up in Chapters 7 and 8. Much attention is focused on the theory that the profit rate has a tendency to fall, which is the exclusive concern of Chapter 7. In Chapter 8 Habermas's other two criticisms are discussed—those concerning collective bargaining and the possibilities of a legitimation crisis.

NOTES

1. *Toward a Rational Society,* p. 114; *Legitimation Crisis,* p. 117ff.

2. *Legitimationsprobleme im Spätkapitalismus* (Frankfurt: Suhrkamp, 1973), p. 34. The English translation is *Legitimation Crisis,* but it omits (cf., p. 19) the quoted sentence.

3. *Legitimation Crisis,* pp. 20-21. The nature of the capital expansion process is discussed in Chapters 5 and 6 of the present study.

4. Ibid., p. 53.

5. Ibid., p. 72.

6. *Theory and Practice,* p. 237.

7. *Legitimation Crisis,* pp. 55-9.

8. Specifically, it is assumed that there is no fixed capital and all components of circulating capital have the same turnover period of one year. It is assumed further that output proportions are such as to allow equation (1) to express accurately the transformation of values into prices of production. These assumptions will be discussed in Chapter 7.

9. Karl Marx, *Capital*, edited by Frederick Engels (3 vols.; New York: International Publishers, 1967), Vol. III, p. 211. If v and s are expressed in terms of units of socially necessary labor time, then they are related to the annually expended living labor k as follows:

$$k = v + s$$

Dividing and then multiplying the right-hand side by v, we can get the following expression:

$$k = (1 + s/v) \, v.$$

Thus if $\frac{s}{v}$ is constant, then k is proportional to v.

10. The relationship between the annually expended living labor k and the number of employed workers may be expressed as follows:

$$k = myz,$$

where m is the average number of employed workers, y the length of the working day in hours, and z the number of working days in the year. If y and z are constant, then k is proportional to m and one can often be used as an index of the other, as has just been done in the text.

11. *Toward a Rational Society*, p. 104.

12. *Legitimation Crisis*, p. 56.

13. "Habermas talking," p. 50. In this interview published in *Theory and Society*, *"reflexive Arbeit"* is rendered as "reflective labor." Since the interview reads as though it were an English translation of an originally German text (although it is not indicated to be such), I have taken the liberty of substituting "reflexive" for "reflective." The former seems more appropriate, since Habermas seems to want to use the expression *"reflexive Arbeit"* not primarily to refer to mental as opposed to manual labor, but rather to refer to the application of the labor process to itself. Thomas McCarthy's translation agrees with mine (cf., *Legitimation Crisis*, p. 56).

14. *Legitimation Crisis*, p. 56.

15. James O'Connor, *The Fiscal Crisis of the State* (New York: St. Martin's, 1973), p. 6.

16. *Legitimation Crisis*, p. 56.

17. Ibid., pp. 56-7.

18. Ibid., p. 57.

19. Ibid.

20. *Capital*, I, p. 171.

21. *Legitimation Crisis*, p. 57.

22. Ibid., p. 52.

23. Ibid., p. 36.

24. Ibid., p. 55.

25. Ibid., p. 36.

26. Ibid., p. 46.

27. See, for example, Pt. II, Ch. 7 of *Legitimation Crisis*.

28. Ibid., pp. 73, 58.

29. Albrecht Wellmer, *Kritische Gesellshaftstheorie und Positivismus* (Frankfurt: Suhrkamp, 1969). I shall refer to the English edition, *Critical Theory of Society*, trans. by John Cumming (New York: Seabury Press, 1974), though I have made alterations in the translation.

30. Speaking of the sphere of communicative interaction, Habermas says: "It is in this very dimension . . . which does not coincide with that of instrumental action, that phenomenological experience moves. In this dimension appear the configurations of consciousness in its manifestations that Marx calls ideology, and in it reifications are dissolved by the silent force of a process of reflection to which Marx gives back the Kantian name of critique" (*Knowledge and Human Interests*, p. 42). Cf., the following passage: "Synthesis through labor brings about a theoretical-technical relation between subject and object; synthesis through struggle brings a theoretical-practical relation between them. Productive knowledge arises in the first, reflective knowledge in the second" (ibid., p. 56).

31. *Knowledge and Human Interests*, pp. 50-51.

32. *Critical Theory of Society*, p. 70.

33. *Grundrisse*, pp. 704-6.

34. *Knowledge and Human Interests*, p. 48.

35. Wellmer, *Critical Theory of Society*, p. 109.

36. For example, see Max Horkheimer and Theodor W. Adorno, *Dialectic of Enlightenment*, trans. by John Cumming (New York: Herder and Herder, 1972) and Herbert Marcuse, *One Dimensional Man* (Boston: Beacon Press, 1964).

37. Habermas, *Toward a Rational Society*, pp. 105-106.

38. Ibid., p. 118.

39. Habermas, *Knowledge and Human Interests*, p. 55.

40. Wellmer, *Critical Theory of Society*, pp. 74-5.

41. *Theory and Practice*, pp. 32ff.

42. *Toward a Rational Society*, p. 58.

43. *Legitimation Crisis*, p. 37. Habermas discusses these theories in, among other places, Pt. III of *Legitimation Crisis* and "The scientization of politics and public opinion," in *Toward a Rational Society*, pp. 62ff.

44. To defend the claim that practical questions can be "decided with reason" (*Legitimation Crisis*, p. 102) is the central motivation behind Habermas's critique of positivism and of noncognitivism in ethics.

Chapter 5

THE CRITIQUE OF POLITICAL ECONOMY

According to Marx, the capitalist process of production has a double character: On the one hand, it is a labor process in which use values are produced. On the other hand, this same labor process has the form of a process of value expansion or capital realization (*Verwertungsprozess des Kapitals*), in which surplus value is produced. This double character of capitalist production is a development of the two-fold nature of commodity-producing labor, the understanding of which, Marx claims, "is the pivot on which a clear comprehension of Political Economy turns."[1] An insufficient appreciation of the point of these claims has been quite common in the history of Marxism,[2] and, in fact, in Chapter 6 I shall argue that Habermas's work does not take due account of their significance. In order to lay a basis for that discussion we shall consider in the present chapter some fundamentals of Marx's critique of political economy.

Commodities and Money

Capitalism is a type of commodity production, and its critical comprehension requires an understanding of the nature of commodities. Commodities are, first of all, use values, or objects of utility. They satisfy human wants of various sorts. Often the same commodity can be used in more than one way, but its various possible uses are limited by and dependent upon its natural properties. For this reason Marx says that "the commodity body itself, such as iron, wheat, diamond, is therefore a use value, a good." It is the existence of the commodity as a natural object which is its existence as a use value.[3] Various standards are used in measuring quantities of use values; e.g., wheat is measured in bushels, linen in yards, and iron in tons.

Regardless of how its production is socially organized, wealth always consists of use values. Thus to say that commodities are use values in no way distinguishes commodity production from any other form of social production. Commodities, however, are not merely use values; in addition, they possess exchange value relative to one another. In so doing, they reveal their socially distinguishing characteristic. For it is only when productive activity is socially organized in a certain way that the products of labor enter into exchange relations with one another.

A commodity can be used to obtain others by means of exchange. The various amounts of the use values thus obtainable each express the exchange value of the commodity. For example, one might express the exchange value of ten yards of linen alternatively as one coat, two shirts, a bushel of wheat, etc. At first sight the proportions in which commodities take each other's place in exchange might appear accidental, without any systematic relation to each other or to anything outside of the exchange process. If this were the case, then nothing more could be said about exchange value than Butler's aphorism, "The value of a thing/Is just as much as it will bring."[4] Value would be purely relative and accidental.

On closer inspection, however, the phenomena of exchange suggest that in being exchangeable for one another, all commodities, despite the diversity of their use values, are commensurable, just as, say, balance scale phenomena indicate a certain commensurability among different physical objects (on the basis of weight). Exchangeability tends to be symmetric, for example. It tends to be the case that if twenty yards of linen "will bring" five shirts (and no more) in exchange, then five shirts will bring twenty yards of linen (and no more). Exchangeability also tends to be transitive: if x will bring y and y will bring z, then x will bring z. These and other market phenomena suggest that there is a relation $E(x,y)$ which holds among commodities (in definite amounts) which expresses equality with respect to a certain extensive magnitude (denote it by "V"). The relation E has the sense of "is worth as much as." For this to be the case, (1) E must be an equivalence relation, (2) a unit for V must be specifiable in terms of E, and (3) V must satisfy a principle of additivity which is consistent with E.[5] We have already indicated the data which support (1), namely the observed symmetry and transitivity among exchange transactions. Condition (2) can be satisfied by specifying one ounce of gold, say, as a unit:

$$V(x) = 1 \text{ if and only if } E(x, 1 \text{ oz. gold}).$$

To satisfy condition (3) we first define "*" as follows: x*y is the commodity consisting of x and y. Thus, for example, 1 yd. linen * 2 oz. gold is the commodity consisting of a yard of linen and two ounces of gold. Now suppose that the following principle held:

If $E(x, \alpha \text{ oz. gold})$ and $E(y, \beta \text{ oz. gold})$,
then $E(x*y, (\alpha + \beta) \text{ oz. gold})$.

Then the following principle of additivity would be satisfied:

$$V(x*y) = V(x) + V(y).$$

Can one argue that these principles hold? Though they are approximated by market phenomena, transaction costs and therefore discounts for buying in large quantities would falsify them for any E which is a mere record of actual exchange. However, the relation E should not be taken as such a record, just as the as-long-as relation should not be taken as a mere record of observations of coincidence behavior of endpoints of intervals. In each case, the relations are constructed via interpretations of the data which involve idealizations and corrections for various intervening factors. The appropriateness of the construction depends in the final analysis on the overall adequacy of the theories which utilize it.[6]

Now the relation which x bears to y when x is as heavy as y cannot partition a set into equivalence classes unless every member of the set has the property of having weight. If the number three is in the set, then the members of the set are not all quantitatively comparable via the as-heavy-as relation. Weight is a quality, expressible in quantitative terms, which each body near the surface of the earth possesses and which is manifested or expressed in the as-heavy-as relation which obtains between certain of these bodies. Similarly, the quantitative comparability of commodities via the exchange-value relation presupposes that all commodities share a common quality. Exchange value "can only be the mode of expression, and 'form of appearance' of a content distinguishable from it," and "the exchange-values of commodities must be capable of being reduced to something common to them all, of which they represent a greater or less quantity." This "common something" is value, a quality possessed by each commodity and expressing itself in the exchange-value relation between commodities.[7]

That exchange value represents a quantity was not discovered by Marx. Classical political economy was primarily concerned with the quantitative aspects of the exchange-value relation and how they are related to techniques of production and patterns of distribution and consumption. Marx too was interested in these questions, but for him they were only part of a larger investigation. Unlike his predecessors, he focused on the question: How is it possible for use values of the most diverse sorts to possess exchange value relative to one another at all? The answer to this question is the distinctively Marxian discovery that value, the quality whose phenomenal form is exchange value, is a purely social property of commodities. Commodities, as values, are not natural, but rather social substances; they are embodiments of certain relations of production.

Insofar as it is a bearer of value, a commodity is exchangeable for a commodity of any other use value whatever. Value, then, is a power possessed by each commodity, a power of transforming, so to speak, its own use value into the use value of any other commodity. A chameleon possesses the ability to change its color, and water can exist as a solid, as a liquid, or as a gas. These features of the chameleon and of water depend upon the natural properties of these two things. The power of metamorphosis possessed by commodities, however, is completely independent of their natural properties. Any two commodities, *regardless* of their use values and thus the natural forms which they happen to possess, are exchangeable for each other, provided they are present in the right proportion. Consequently, value is not a natural property of commodities; "not an atom of natural matter [*Naturstoff*] enters into its composition."[8] Rather, the value of commodities "has a purely social reality"; it is given to them not by nature but by society, albeit unconsciously, as we shall see.

Products of labor possess value when and only when production has a certain social form, viz., that of a social division of labor in which individuals or groups of individuals work privately and independently of one another. Such a society is characterized by the absence of any authoritative, intersubjectively acknowledged social organization of the production process; instead, decisions concerning the whats and hows of production are made privately and independently of one another. Labor in this society is in the first instance private; that it is also social is not something which can be ascertained or verified at the stage of production.

That the various laboring activities of the producers in this society together constitute the expenditure of the labor power expended by society for the satisfaction of social needs is manifested only by the mutual exchangeability of the producers' products. In other words, in order for social production by private producers to take place, the products of labor must be not only use values but also bearers of value.

By contrast, when the process of production does not take the form of social labor carried on privately and independently, the products of labor are not commodities; they are use values but not values. For example, in a primitive hunting and gathering society there is a spontaneously developed division of labor, as in commodity production. However, in this case laboring activities of the various individuals are immediate social functions; that they form part of the total labor of society is known from the start and is not verified in an exchange process. The rabbits killed by a hunter are not his private property which he can use to "shop around" and bargain for other items; rather, they belong immediately to the community and are distributed on the basis of mechanisms other than an exchange process (largely ritually, in accordance with tradition or religion). Hence in this society the products of labor do not have that peculiar nonnatural power of metamorphosis, value. They are not commodities.

Whenever individuals work for one another, their labor has a social character. The nature of this character and how it manifests itself, however, vary from society to society. In a society of individuals carrying on their work with the means of production held in common, for example, the social character of labor might take the form of conscious, collective planning and execution of the production process. In a commodity-producing society, however, the social character of labor takes the form, not of direct social relations among the producers, but of a material or objective (*sachlich*) quality of the products of labor. This quality, value, is an expression of the social character of private labor carried on independently. On the basis of the fact that it expresses itself as value, more can be said about the specific nature of this social character. It is to this task that we now turn.

Since commodities are use values, commodity producing labor must be useful labor, i.e., labor whose result is the existence of an object with useful properties. This requires that the labor be of a definite sort. For example, linen cloth owes its existence as a useful object to the fact that it results from the combination of specific materials (e.g., linen yarn, a loom) with productive activity which has a specific aim and mode of operation. Since commodity production involves a division of labor, there will be many different kinds of commodity-producing labor, each of which finds expression in a different use value.

As productive of value, on the other hand, these activities are essentially of the same kind. Since commodities, as values, are qualitatively identical, so must be the various commodity-producing activities, insofar as they find expression in value. As values, commodities are all material expressions of the *same* labor. Consequently, in order to express themselves in value, the various concrete laboring activities must be reduced to labor of the same kind. Such a reduction can only take place by means of an abstraction from the qualitative differences in these activities. This abstraction is executed in the exchange process. The exchange of commodities, insofar as it equates them as bearers of value, abstracts from all their various useful properties; in so doing, it also abstracts from the specific productive modes in which the labor embodied in them was performed. All of these various kinds of labor are reduced to what is common to them all: human labor in the abstract.

In other words, the various laboring activities of different individuals have something in common: they all possess the property of being human labor. In the production of value, this general feature is the only thing that counts. Weaving creates the value of linen, for example, not by virtue of being weaving, but solely by virtue of its general property of being human labor. In commodity production the weaver's labor becomes social labor only through its reduction to universal or homogenous labor, i.e., labor qualitatively identical to the labor of every other individual. The only difference remaining is a quantitative one, which determines differences in the magnitude of value of the various commodities. In this respect the social character of commodity-producing labor distinguishes itself from that of labor in other social formations.

Within the patriarchal industry of a peasant family, for instance, weaving in its concrete form as weaving is a directly social activity, "because the individual labor powers operate from the start only as organs of the common labor power of the family."[9] In contrast to commodity production, in which the concrete activities of laboring individuals are immediately private and only indirectly social (through their reduction to abstract labor), the immediate social form of labor is in this case its concrete form.

In all societies the labor of the individual must, as a definite useful kind of labor, hold its place as a component part of the labor of society. In some societies the labor of the individual satisfies this requirement directly, on the basis of its concrete form. In commodity production, however, a mediation is necessary. The labor of the individual is in the first instance private and manifests its social character only through the exchangeability of its product. In order to be exchangeable, the product must be a use value, and its use value manifests the useful character of the labor embodied in it. However, in order to be exchangeable, it must also have value; otherwise, the producer could not get anything in exchange for his product. The value of the product results from the reduction of the labor of the individual to human labor in the abstract. Hence, commodity-producing labor has a two-fold social character: as in all societies, it must reveal itself as useful labor of a definite kind, but as social labor peculiar to commodity production, it must take the form of human labor in the abstract.

> On the one hand, it must, as a definite useful kind of labor, satisfy a definite social want, and thus hold its place as part and parcel of the collective labor of all, as a branch of the social division of labor that has sprung up spontaneously. On the other hand, it can satisfy the manifold wants of the individual producer himself, only in so far as the mutual exchangeability of all kinds of useful private labor is an established social fact, and therefore the private useful labor of each producer ranks on an equality with that of all the others. The equalization of the most different kinds of labor can be the result only of an abstraction from their inequalities, or of reducing them to their common denominator, viz., expenditure of human labor power or human labor in the abstract.[10]

Every laboring activity may be regarded, on the one hand, as having a certain concrete form responsible for giving its product a definite use value, and, on the other hand, as having the general property of being human labor. It might seem, therefore, that in any society labor has the two-fold nature described above and consequently that the concept of value is applicable to all forms of society. To draw this conclusion, however, would be fundamentally to misunderstand Marx's theory of value.[11] In some societies, specifically those in which the concrete form of labor is the immediate social form, the equating of all laboring activities by virtue of their property of being human labor could only be a process of mental generalization, perhaps on the part of a social scientist or a production planner. The result of this process of abstraction is a concept, the object of which does not attain an existence independent of the various concrete laboring activities. In commodity production, however, the reduction of concrete laboring activities to human labor in the abstract is in the first instance not a process of mental generalization at all but rather a real social process effected unconsciously by the social intercourse among commodity producers.

Human beings . . . do not relate the products of their labor to one
another as values because those objects are regarded by them as
merely material receptacles of homogenous human labor. Just the
reverse. By equating their varied products as values in exchange, they
equate their different labors as human labor. They are not aware of
this, but they do it.[12]

Abstract labor, as value, attains an existence distinct from the various
concrete laboring activities. For example, in contrast to social formations
in which social labor time is merely the sum of the periods which
individuals spend working, social labor time and individual labor time
diverge from each other in commodity production. This circumstance
arises from the fact that social labor which takes the form of a material
quality of the products of labor must be present in identical products to
the same degree, regardless of any differences in the times individuals
actually take to produce them.

The determination of exchange-value by labor time . . . presupposes
that the *same amount* of labor is materialized in a particular commodity, say a ton of iron, irrespective of whether it is the work of A
or B, i.e., that different individuals spend equal amounts of labor-
time to produce use-values which are qualitatively and quantitatively
equal. In other words, it is presupposed that the labor-time contained in a commodity is the labor-time *necessary* for its production,
namely the labor time required, under the generally prevailing conditions of production, to produce a new specimen of the same commodity.[13]

Thus the introduction of productivity-increasing technical innovations can
reduce the amount of social labor involved in transforming a given quantity of raw materials into products, in spite of the fact that producers
working under the old conditions still require the same amount of time as
before.

The introduction of power-looms into England probably reduced by
one-half the labor required to weave a given quantity of yarn into
cloth. The hand loom weavers, as a matter of fact, continued to
require the same time as before; but for all that, the product of one
hour of their labor represented after the change only half an hour's
social labor, and consequently fell to one-half its former value.[14]

Thus laboring activities which produce commodities have a two-fold
character not merely in the sense that they can be considered by the

investigator from two points of view—on the one hand as various specific kinds of productive activity and on the other as human labor—but also—and especially—in the sense that these two aspects of labor diverge from one another in the social process of production itself and stand in opposition to each other.

> The *same* labor is determined differently and even contrarily according to whether it is related to the *use value* of the commodity as its *product* or to the *commodity-value* as its merely *objectified* expression.[15]

This contradiction between use value and value, between concrete and abstract labor, is, of course, a consequence of the fact that commodity-producing labor is *social* labor by *private* individuals. No production technique is accorded social validity in advance; the social character of production is constituted as a result of many privately made decisions and is revealed only after the fact, in the exchange process.

> Social labor time exists so to speak only latently in . . . commodities and reveals itself only in their exchange process. The point of departure is not the labor of individuals as communal labor but the reverse, namely the particular labors of private individuals, labors which prove themselves as universal social labor only through the suspension [*Aufhebung*] of their original character in the exchange process. Universal social labor is therefore not a ready-made prerequisite but an emerging result.[16]

Commodity producers are compelled, under penalty of losing their share in the distribution of the social product, to pay attention to the social character of their labor, as it is expressed in the exchangeability of their products. The inability to sell a product at all or only at a reduced price is a sign that some change in product or in technique of production is called for. However, since the different producers or groups of producers do not come into social contact with each other until the exchange process, changes in value or in price, which determine the extent to which their labor counts as social labor, take place independently of their will, in spite of the fact that these changes are brought about as a result of their own actions. Hence, since they nevertheless must accommodate themselves to these changes, commodity producers belong to a society in which their own process of production has control over them rather than the other way around. Commodity-producing labor, therefore, is essentially alienated labor. The products of that labor, as values, and that labor itself, as value creating, function independently of the intentions of the producers, determining their activity rather than being its conscious creation.

Although value is an expression of specific social relations of production, the mistaken notion that it is an eternally valid category has a basis in commodity production itself. For the mastery of commodity production over commodity producers proceeds in such a manner that it seems to result from the nature of the products *as natural objects*. A fetish character thus attaches itself to commodities; that is to say, they seem to possess their social powers by nature, completely independently of the way production is socially organized.

This fetish character is a necessary by-product of commodity-producing labor. As we have seen, the specific social character of private laboring activities carried on independently consists in their equality as human labor and takes the form of an objective character of the products of labor, namely their character as values. Commodities, then, have an objective form as bearers of value. They do not, however, assume this form in isolation from one another. Twenty yards of linen, for example, do not have embroidered on them that they are a congelation of so many hours of abstract social labor. Nor do any of the natural properties of the linen express its character as a bearer of value; they do not distinguish it from its counterpart in other forms of society but merely reveal its character as a use value. The value form of the linen, the form which it assumes as value, must be different from its natural form. That it is a bearer of value is revealed, along with the magnitude of that value, only in its social relations with other commodities, i.e., only in the exchange-value relation. The value of the linen can be expressed only relatively, in terms of some other commodity, for example as follows:

20 yards of linen are worth 1 coat.

The necessity for value to find this sort of expression lies at the root of the seemingly natural (and hence eternal) character of value. For in this expression, the value of linen is expressed in terms of coats. The value of one commodity is expressed in terms of the use value of another. When brought into this relation with the linen, the coat, in its bodily form as a natural object, serves as the material in which the value of the linen is expressed. In this way the appearance arises that value is some kind of natural substance, for it seems that the coat possesses its ability to express value solely by virtue of its natural properties. It seems to be endowed with its property of being exchangeable with the linen "just as much by nature as it is endowed with the property of being heavy, or the capacity to keep us warm."[17] That a specific social relation of production lies behind and is expressed in value is thereby masked over. "Value . . . does not stalk about with a label describing what it is. It is value, rather, that converts every product into a social hieroglyphic."[18]

The Marxian theory of value deciphers this hieroglyphic. The significance of this achievement must not be misunderstood. The theory explains why value, which has a purely social reality, must express itself in terms of a natural material and hence seems to be a natural substance. Classical political economy took this semblance for truth and treated the representation of labor by value as a nature-imposed necessity. The critique of political economy exposes this error by bringing to light the nature of value as an expression of certain specific social relations of production. It does not, however, remove the false semblance, any more than an understanding of the laws of refraction destroys mirages. The semblance of value as a natural property, the fetishism of commodities, is inseparable from commodity production.[19] It results, as we have seen, from the necessity of the social character of commodity-producing labor to take the form of an objective property of the products of that labor. No theoretical understanding is sufficient to remove this necessity.

Marx calls the expression of the value of one commodity in terms of a single other commodity chosen at random the *elementary form of value:*[20]

x commodity A is worth y commodity B
20 yards of linen are worth 1 coat

He argues that the seed for the development of money is inherent in this elementary form. The fundamental tenet of Marx's theory of money is that money is an expression of the social relations of commodity production. It arises out of the necessity, explained above, for each commodity to find a value form distinct from its natural form. To express the commodity as bearer of value in an adequate manner, the value form must express the nature of the commodity as a congelation of undifferentiated human labor and therefore as qualitatively equal and quantitatively proportional to all other commodities. The elementary form expresses value, but inadequately; the value relation does not yet expressly encompass the entire world of commodities. In the third section of the opening chapter of *Capital*, Marx considers four forms of value and argues that only the last—the money form, or the expression of the value of all commodities in terms of a single commodity, which thereby takes on the role of money—is adequate to express value. We shall not retrace the argument here. Suffice it to say that Marx presents the four forms as successive developments of the elementary form, which is inherent in the exchange of one commodity for another. In this way he argues that money expresses a social relation of production and is an inherent development of commodity production.

Thus, as a result of the reified character of the social relations of commodity production, i.e., the necessity of commodity-producing labor to express its peculiar social character in the form of a property of the products of that labor, a social relation of production parades around in money in the form of a thing. The commodity which assumes the role of money becomes the universal equivalent of all commodities; it is the universal incarnation of abstract social labor. The fetish character of commodities thus assumes a particularly striking form in money.

Capital

When circumstances permit money to be advanced in the purchase and sale of commodities in such a manner as to yield an increment in value, then we have the transformation of money into *capital*, i.e., into value which is self-expanding. The increment which money advanced as capital yields is called *surplus* value.

If the transformation of money into capital is to be explained under the assumption of exchange of equivalents, and according to Marx it cannot be attributed to any divergence from equivalent exchange,[21] then the would-be capitalist must be able to buy commodities at their value, sell them at their value, and yet end up with more value than he started with. This apparently paradoxical process is made possible by the existence of labor power as a commodity. This commodity has the specific use value of being a source not only of value, but of more value than it has itself. Its own value is determined by the labor time socially necessary for the production of its means of subsistence. Its ability to be set to work for a period longer than this amount of time is what renders the creation of surplus value possible. In order to expand his capital, the capitalist need merely purchase labor power and means of production at their value, apply the labor power to the means of production for a period of time longer than that necessary to reproduce the value of the labor power, and then sell the resulting commodities at their value. The value of the means of production used up in the production process is simply transferred to the produced commodities. To this value the workers, by means of their labor, add not only value, but more value than was paid to them for the purchase of their labor power. In this way, they produce the surplus value appropriated by the capitalist.

Capitalism generalizes commodity production, turning it into the most universal form of social production. Hence the categories of the theory of value apply to capitalist production par excellence.[22] Nevertheless, capitalism is a *specific form* of commodity production, one founded on the separation of the producers from the means of production and the consequent existence of labor power as a commodity. For this reason the contradictions of commodity production take on in capitalism more specific, further developed forms than the abstract ones just presented. Thus the production process, considered simply as a process of commodity production, is the labor process in its two-fold character as a process of both use-value and value production; considered as the capitalist production of commodities, however, it becomes the labor process in its two-fold character as a process of both use value and *surplus* value production. In other words, the contradiction between concrete and abstract labor takes on in capitalism the more specific form of the contradiction between the process of producing use values and the process of producing surplus value.

Marx calls the process of producing surplus value the "*Verwertungsprozess des Kapitals*," a term which has been translated in the present study alternatively as "value expansion process of capital" and "capital expansion process." He speaks of the production process in capitalism as the unity of the labor process and the value expansion process. This manner of speaking might lead one to suppose that for Marx the value expansion process is not itself a labor process but some other type of process. This would be a mistake. When Marx opposes the value expansion process to the labor process, he is thinking of the latter insofar as it is concrete useful labor, productive of use value. The value expansion process is the same labor process, however, insofar as it is abstract, surplus value producing labor. The value expansion process is the specific social form which the labor process assumes in capitalism. Thus the production process is the *immediate* (though contradictory) unity of the labor process and the value expansion process:

> If we consider the production process from two different points of view 1) as *labor process*, 2) as *value-expansion process*, then it is implied that it is only a single, indivisible labor process. It is not executed twice, one time in order to create a useful product, a use value . . . and another time to create surplus value, to expand value.[23]

Capital is value in a process of self-expansion. In the course of this process it takes on many forms: money, means of production and labor power, the immediate production process itself, commodities, money again (this time in greater quantity), means of production and labor power again, and so on.[24] The specific use value which labor power possesses in this process is its property of being a source of surplus value. The consumption of this use value is the capitalist process of production.[25] In this process, as in all forms of social production, use values are produced. However, this process of production distinguishes itself from all others in that the production of use values must take the form of the production of surplus value. The production of use values is in fact here a mere sine qua non, for in order to create value, labor must be useful labor. The labor process in capitalism is a mere means toward the goal of expansion of the value which the capitalist has advanced in the form of capital.

In the production process, the capitalist acts as master, but he has this role only insofar as he is capital personified. Value expansion forms the ruling principle, and just as little as commodity producers in general have control over the requirements of value production does the capitalist set the requirements of value expansion.[26] These requirements are set behind his back, independently of his conscious will. Their dictates range from the length and intensity of the labor process to its specific technical features. If he fails to satisfy them, then he will go bankrupt, and his capital will pass into the hands of someone who will use it properly. In capitalism it is neither the capitalist nor the worker who controls the conditions of production but the conditions of production which control them. Of course, the capitalist is more likely to feel at home in this alienated condition than the worker. The productive powers of social labor are developed in opposition to living labor power as a means of extracting surplus value from it; they are developed as the power of objectified labor to expand itself at the expense of living labor. Thus capital, like value, or rather precisely because it is value in a process of self-expansion, is a social relation of production which takes the form of a property of a thing.

The specific form which this process of reification takes in capitalism increases the mystification inherent in the commodity form.[27] The necessity for capital in the course of its self-expansion to take the form of the means of production and even of the production process itself as modes of its own existence gives rise to the appearance that the means of production are capital *by nature* and that the production of use values is inherently capitalistic.

On the basis of capitalist production this capacity of objectified labor to transform itself into *capital*, i.e., to transform the means of production into means of the command over and the exploitation of living labor, appears as belonging to these means of production in and of themselves ... as inseparable from them, thus as *properties which they possess as things, as use values, as means of production.*[28]

NOTES

1. *Capital,* I, p. 41.

2. Wolfgang Müller and Christel Neusüss argue that the inability to grasp the production process as the contradictory unity of the labor process and the value expansion process is "common to revisionism since Bernstein." "Die Sozialstaatsillusion und der Widerspruch von Lohnarbeit und Kapital," *Probleme des Klassenkampfs,* Sonderheft 1 (June 1971): 17. A translation of this article appears in *Telos* No. 25 (Fall 1975): 13-90, but it contains serious inaccuracies and should not be relied upon. For example, on p. 24 we find the following sentences: "Every production process is also a labor process. Independent of the relations of production, it is the performance of useful labor with the purpose of producing commodities." The use of "commodities" here as a translation of "Gebrauchsgüter" has Müller and Neusüss asserting that commodity production is eternal, which is something they are quite concerned to deny. A better translation would be "use values" or "useful items." I am not concerned here to endorse all the claims made in this article, but the authors do appreciate the significance of the double character of capitalist production—a fact which is concealed by errors in translation such as this one.

3. *Capital,* I, p. 36. See also p. 27 of Marx's *A Contribution to the Critique of Political Economy* (Moscow:Progress Publishers, 1970): "Use value as an aspect of the commodity coincides with the physical, palpable existence of the commodity."

4. Samuel Butler, quoted by Marx in *Capital,* I, p. 36, n.4.

5. Rudolf Carnap, *Philosophical Foundations of Physics* (New York: Basic Books, 1966), Ch. 7. See also Carl G. Hempel, *Fundamentals of Concept Formation in Empirical Science,* Vol. II, No. 7 of the *International Encyclopedia of Unified Science,* ed. by Otto Neurath (Chicago: University of Chicago Press, 1952), Pt. III.

6. For clarification of some of the issues discussed in this paragraph, I am indebted to Mark Kaplan and John Bennett.

7. *Capital,* I, p. 37. Helpful in connection with the ideas expressed in this and the preceding paragraph is the critique of the superficial relativism of Samuel Bailey in Marx's *Theories of Surplus Value,* Pt. III, trans. by Jack Cohen and S.W. Ryazanskaya (Moscow: Progress Publishers, 1971), pp. 124-67. "If I say that the area of the triangle A is equal to that of the parallelogram B, this means not only that the area of the triangle is expressed in the parallelogram and that of the parallelogram in the triangle, but it means that if the height of the triangle is equal to h and the base equal to b, then $A = (h \times b)/2$, a property which belongs to it itself just as it is a property of the parallelogram that it is likewise equal to $(h \times b)/2$. As areas, the triangle and the parallelogram are here declared to be equal, to be equivalents, although as a triangle and a parallelogram they are different. In order to equate these different things with one another, each must represent *the same common element* regardless of the other. If geometry, like the political economy of Mr. Bailey,

contented itself with saying that the equality of the triangle and the parallelogram means that the triangle is expressed in the parallelogram and the parallelogram in the triangle, it would be of little value" (pp. 143-4 n.).

8. *Capital*, I, p. 47.
9. Ibid., p. 78.
10. Ibid., p. 73.
11. For an account of how persistent such a misunderstanding has been even on the part of Marxists, see Marc Linder's *Reification and the Consciousness of the Critics of Political Economy: Sudies in the Development of Marx's Thoery of Value* (Ph.D. dissertation, Princeton University, 1973; published in Copenhagen by Rhodos International Science and Art Publishers, 1975). See also the essay by Lucio Colletti, "Bernstein and the Marxism of the Second International," in his *From Rousseau to Lenin*, trans. by John Merrington and Judith White (New York and London: Monthly Review Press, 1972).
12. *Capital*, I, p. 74.
13. Marx, *A Contribution to the Critique of Political Economy*, p. 31.
14. *Capital*, I, p. 39.
15. *Das Kapital* (1st ed., 1867), cited according to reprint of the first chapter in Marx/Engels, *Studienausgabe*, ed. by I. Fetscher, II (Frankfurt, 1966) p. 224.
16. *Contribution to the Critique of Political Economy*, p. 45.
17. *Capital*, I, p. 57.
18. Ibid., p. 74.
19. Ibid., p. 18.
20. Ibid., p. 48
21. See *Capital*, I, Ch. V, entitled "Contradictions in the general formula of capital."
22. "Only when and where wage-labor is its basis does commodity production impose itself upon society as a whole; but only then and there does it unfold all its hidden potentialities" (*Capital*, I, p. 587).
23. Marx, *Resultate des unmittelbaren Produktionsprozesses* (Frankfurt: Verlag Neue Kritik, 1974), p. 19. See also *Capital*, I, p. 195: "If we proceed further and compare the process of value creation with the labor process, we find that the latter consists of the useful labor which produces use values. The movement is here qualitatively considered, in its special manner of operation as regards its end and content. The *same labor process* represents itself in the value-creation process under its quantitative aspect alone" (emphasis added).
24. See *Capital*, II, Pt. I.
25. The view is often attributed to Marx that use value lies outside the sphere of investigation of political economy. This is inaccurate. Marx's view is that use value lies outside that sphere *insofar as it is indifferent to the determination of economic form*. Where it enters into that determination, it is a proper subject of political-economic investigation. In the value form of commodities, for example "use value is the immediate physical entity in which a definite economic relationship—*exchange value* —is expressed" (*Contribution to the Critique of Political Economy*, p. 28). The use value of labor power as a source of surplus value provides a case in which "the consumption of the use value itself . . . falls within the economic process, because the use value here is itself determined by exchange value. In no moment of the production process does capital cease to be capital or value to be value." (*Grundrisse*, p. 311). Just as value is expressed through the natural properties of the money

commodity, so is the self-expansion process of capital realized through the material-technical features of the production process. And just as commodity production tends to select a money commodity whose natural features are appropriate to express value, so does capitalism foster the development of technical features of production which are appropriate for value expansion. These aspects of Marx's theory of capital will come under detailed consideration in the next chapter. They are quite important in connection with the question of the political "neutrality" of technology. For a helpful discussion of Marx's conception of the role of use value in political economy, see Roman Rosdolsky's "K. Marx und das Problem des Gebrauchswerts in der politischen Ökonomie," which appears as Ch. 3 of his *Zur Entstehungsgeschichte des Marxschen "Kapital"* (2 vols.; Frankfurt: Europäische Verlagsanstalt, 1968). The book has recently been translated into English as *The Making of Marx's Capital* (New York: Urizen Books, 1977).

26. "Only as personified capital is the capitalist respectable. As such, he shares with the miser the passion for wealth as wealth. But that which in the miser is a mere idiosyncrasy is in the capitalist the operation [*Wirkung*] of the social mechanism, of which he is but one of the wheels" (*Capital*, I, p. 592).

27. See *Capital*, III, pp. 826-7; and Marx, *Theories of Surplus Value*, Pt. I, trans. by Emile Burns (Moscow: Progress Publishers, 1963), pp. 389-92.

28. *Resultate des unmittelbaren Produktionsprozesses*, pp. 16-7.

Chapter 6

HISTORICAL MATERIALISM

The reader will recall from Ch. 4, pp. 68-75 that Habermas and Wellmer are concerned to point out a tension in Marx's theoretical work between ideology-critical and technocratic approaches. According to this claim, in the critique of political economy Marx "takes account of social practice that encompasses both work and interaction."[1] Here we have the "official"[2] Marx, sensitive to the problem of ideology and enlightenment, thereby acknowledging that production and socialization are distinct dimensions of social evolution and consequently that practical rationalization and technical rationalization are logically independent of each other. This acknowledgment, however, remains implicit, because the critique of political economy is overlaid with "a philosophical self-understanding restricted to the categorical framework of production."[3] That is, Marx's conceptualization of the process of societal reproduction is due to a technocratic philosophy of history which he inappropriately uses as a philosophical foundation for his "material investigations."[4] The foundation is inappropriate because it fails to appreciate the irreducible difference between work and interaction and consequently identifies progress with technical rationalization. Habermas and Wellmer refer to this supposed technocratic strain in Marx's work as "positivist" both because of its Saint-Simonian character and because Habermas's epistemology ties it to a regard for the physical sciences as the paradigm of knowledge. Indeed, Habermas claims that because of this strain, Marx mistakenly assimilates his own theory to natural science. This assimilation, the reader will recall, is allegedly responsible for an objectivistic concept of revolution which in the history of the socialist movement has led both to technocratic-elitist conceptions of the revolutionary party and to quietism.

In my opinion, this characterization of Marx's work as tension-ridden by conflicting approaches is incorrect, and not simply because it asserts the existence of a technocratic strain which is not there. We shall discuss the conceptualization of the process of societal reproduction which Marx employs in the construction of his critique of political economy, and I shall argue that Habermas misunderstands *both* the conceptualization *and* the critique. If the analysis is correct, then not only is Marx's conceptualization not technocratic; it is also crucial to the ideology-critical claims he wants to make, so that the critique of political economy cannot be reconstructed in Habermas's quite different conceptual framework without essential loss. In arguing for these claims, I shall try to go beyond issues of correct textual interpretation to point out certain features of Habermas's approach which lead to errors in the analysis of modern capitalism.

Clarification of Issues

Let us begin by trying to formulate in a fairly precise way the charge that Marx tries to reduce socialization to production. Let $[p_1, \ldots, p_n]$ be a set of variables which are sufficient for an adequate characterization of production, and suppose further that each p_i is an essential member of this set—that is, no proper subset of $[p_1, \ldots, p_n]$ is sufficient for an adequate characterization of production. What "adequate characterization" means will be discussed in a moment. Let $[s_1, \ldots, s_m]$ be a corresponding set of variables for socialization. (Of course, not all of these variables need be quantifiable.) Then a reduction of socialization to production, at least in one fairly straightforward sense, would be a specification of functions $f_1, \ldots, f_m$ such that

$$s_1 = f_1(p_1, \ldots, p_n)$$
$$.$$
$$.$$
$$.$$
$$s_m = f_m(p_1, \ldots, p_n)$$

The existence of such functions would mean that for every set of values for $p_1, \ldots, p_n$ there is a unique set of values for $s_1, \ldots, s_m$, though not necessarily vice versa. In such a situation, a minimal set of predicates which would suffice to characterize the state of the production process at a given time would also suffice to characterize the state of the socialization process at the time.[5]

As far as I can tell, Habermas and Wellmer have something like this in mind when they charge Marx with attempting to reduce socialization to production—at least in some formulations of the charge. Now one should note that reduction in this sense becomes a trivially satisfiable requirement if one is allowed to define production arbitrarily: one could then just stipulate that the socialization variables $s_1, \ldots, s_m$ were among the production variables $p_1, \ldots, p_n$. But of course then one would not really have carried out a reduction of socialization to *production,* but only to something which one has arbitrarily defined as production. Habermas claims that this is precisely what Marx does: "The only way Marx salvages production as the independent variable is by terminological equivocation .... The concept of production is given such a broad meaning that even the relations of production are implied by it." A little later, he continues: "These definitional attempts to subsume all aspects of social practice under the concept of production cannot conceal that Marx has to take account of social preconditions of production that, unlike the material, instruments, energy, and organization of labor, do not belong immediately to the labor process itself."[6] Habermas is referring to remarks which Marx makes in the Introduction to the *Grundrisse* concerning the relationship between production and the social relations in which it takes place:

> [B]efore distribution can be the distribution of products, it is (1) the distribution of the instruments of production, and (2), which is a further specification of the same relation, the distribution of the members of the society among the different kinds of production. (Subsumption of the individuals under specific relations of production.) The distribution of products is evidently only a result of this distribution, which is comprised within the process of production itself and determines the structure of production. To examine production while disregarding this internal distribution within it is obviously an empty abstraction; while conversely, the distribution of products follows by itself from this distribution which forms an original moment of production.[7]

Habermas thinks that one can give an adequate characterization of production without using interactional variables. For him, production proceeds solely according to the rules of instrumental and strategic action; rules of communicative action pertain to the sphere of distribution but not that of production.[8] Of course, production cannot go on—at least in a regular, stable manner—without being "embedded" in an institutional framework or interactional context. But this fact is merely a matter of the causal interdependence of production and socialization. Though the result may not be stable, it is always logically or conceptually possible to detach a given labor process from its interactional context and to embed it in a new one. Now Habermas sees Marx as simply broadening this concept of production to include interactional elements in order to reconcile his historical materialism, which treats societal reproduction as production, with his critique of political economy, which implicitly recognizes both purposive-rational action and symbolic interaction as logically independent factors in societal reproduction.

This charge is justifiable only if it can be shown that Marx includes in his concept of production elements which do not really belong there. It is certainly true that Marx incorporates interactional elements in his concept of production. However, it seems to me that this conceptualization is not a misinterpretation of his material investigations but rather is quite warranted by them. As we shall see below, the critique of political economy views labor and interaction as sometimes internally related, in which case a change in interactional context would involve essential changes in the labor process. Consequently, Marx's individuation of stages in the development of production is fundamentally different from that provided by Habermas's concept of technical rationalization. For Habermas, the historical development of production is something describable apart from production's various interactional contexts (though these contexts may be causally relevant to that development). For Marx, on the other hand, interactional contexts are viewed as social forms of the production process. The historical development of production is not something describable in abstraction from these forms; rather it is precisely the assumption and shedding of these forms by the production process.

Since Marx claims that production cannot be adequately characterized apart from interaction, the claim that he is trying to reduce interaction to production is somewhat misleading. Certainly he is not trying to reduce interaction to Habermas's concept of production. A debate over whether A is reducible to B ought to proceed on the basis of a concept of B which is shared by all parties. Such a basis is lacking here. This is the first issue which must be settled in the debate between Marx and Habermas: can production be adequately characterized apart from interaction? And it is a crucial issue. Suppose it can be shown, as I shall argue below, that Marx's conceptualization reveals certain very important features about production which cannot be captured by Habermas's approach. Then Habermas can still claim, as he is very concerned to do, that there are certain important features about *interaction* which Marx's approach cannot grasp. But the plausibility of this claim will be weakened to the extent that Habermas continues to base it on his own faulty conceptualization of the relation between production and interaction.

But Habermas would not want to retain his conceptualization—at least not without modification. To see this, a final preliminary clarification is necessary. The central issue is what is involved in an adequate characterization of production. If the debate is not to proceed at cross purposes, then it must be oriented toward mutually acknowledged criteria of adequacy. This requirement, it turns out, is not hard to satisfy. Habermas wants to develop a framework for a theory which is sensitive to what is involved in the formation and dissolution of power relations between classes and ideological supports thereof. He is also concerned to bring to light the ideological nature of technocratic consciousness, especially as expressed in the view that all remaining social problems are purely technical ones. It is for precisely these reasons that he criticizes Marx's historical materialism. Let these aims provide the criteria of adequacy. I think it can be shown that, ironically, Marx's conceptualization is more adequate to the achievement of these aims than that of Habermas.

The Real Subsumption of Labor Under Capital

Possibly the most important categories in Marx's conceptualization of the process of societal reproduction in his critique of political economy are those of form and content. Societal reproduction involves both communicative interaction and production. For Marx, however, these two processes do not develop in distinct dimensions, each with its own developmental logic; rather, interaction is related to production as form to content. Productive activity—the purposive creation of use values—always has a certain social form given by the relations of production. For example, in commodity production use values are produced as values, i.e., as congelations of abstract social labor, and thus the production process must assume the form of a process of producing value. Capitalist production is a specific type of commodity production, one in which wealth is produced in the form of commodities which are bearers not only of value, but also of surplus value. Thus the production process in capitalism has the specific social form of a process of value expansion. Thus he often speaks of capital as a social form and of the production process as the content of this form.[9]

Hegel points out that the categories of form and content may be used to grasp both external and internal relations:

> The essential point to keep in mind about the opposition of Form and Content is that the content is not formless, but has the form in its own self, quite as much as the form is external to it. There is thus a doubling of form. At one time it is . . . identical with the content. At another time it is . . . the external existence, which does not at all affect the content.

An example of an external relation of form to content is the relation between the form of a book, conceived of as the type of printing and binding, and the content conceived of as the ideas expressed in the book. Here "it certainly has no bearing upon the content, whether [the book] be written or printed, bound in paper or in leather." Hegel speaks of poetry as providing a clear example of a "thorough-going identity" or an internal relation between form and content. We usually conceive of the content of a poem as the thought or sentiment expressed and the form as being determined by the words employed, the versification, the meter, and so on. But in this case what the content *is* depends on the form in which it is expressed. A different form would entail a different content. Thus "the content of Romeo and Juliet may . . . be said to be the ruin of two lovers through the discord between their families: but something more is needed to make Shakespeare's immortal tragedy."[10]

Now Marx was very concerned to bring to light the establishment of certain internal relations between capital and the production process. The historical onset of capitalism does not immediately require such relations. For example, the transformation of independent commodity producers into wage laborers often did not immediately involve any essential changes in the labor process itself. In these circumstances, the labor process is merely *formally* subjected to capital. Although the labor process has become a means for the value expansion process, it still bears only an external relation to its capitalist form. Nothing about the way the labor process takes place marks it as a specifically capitalist labor process. It is still quite compatible with other relations of production. This merely formal subsumption, however, sets in motion a process of transformation which Marx calls the *real* subsumption of labor under capital.[11] This process turns the exploitation of labor by capital into a necessary ingredient of the labor process itself. An internal relation is established between the labor process and its form as a value expansion process. It would not be the same (type of) labor process if it did not have a capitalist form.

Especially important in bringing about the real subsumption of labor under capital is the development of techniques of producing relative surplus value—techniques of production which increase surplus labor time through the curtailment of necessary labor time.[12] The first step in this development is the acquisition by the labor process of a cooperative character. Marx defines cooperation as follows: "When numerous laborers work together side by side, whether in one and the same process, or in different but connected processes, they are said to cooperate, or to work in cooperation."[13] It is important to realize that cooperation is something over and above the assemblage of workers in a single place. This assemblage is a necessary but not sufficient condition for cooperation. Cooperation is labor *in common*; it is *coordinated* activity. Coordination will thus be present in any cooperative labor process, regardless of whether the relations of production are capitalist or noncapitalist. Within capitalism, however, this coordination acquires special characteristics: it must be guided by the requirements of value expansion and thus must be used so as to further the exploitation of labor by capital.

Marx claims that cooperation, if it involves large numbers of workers, requires a directing authority:

> All combined labor on a large scale requires, more or less, a directing authority, in order to secure the harmonious working of the individual activities, and to perform the general functions that have their origin in the combined organism, as distinguished from the action of its separate organs. A single violin player is his own conductor; an orchestra requires a separate one.[14]

The capacity of individuals to cooperate is a productive force. A directing authority is a purely technical feature of cooperative labor on a large scale in the sense that it is a necessary condition for any productive activity, capitalist or noncapitalist, which utilizes this productive force by a large number of workers. Within capitalism, however, this authority accrues to the capitalist. It must therefore be exercised by him or by someone else in his interests. If this authority is not used "properly"—i.e., so as to further the process of value expansion—then the enterprise will not succeed economically. Thus the capital-labor relation must realize and express itself through a specific determination of the labor process itself. A directing authority performing capitalist exploitation functions becomes something the labor process needs in order to be carried on. In this way the mode of production becomes specifically capitalist; the labor process becomes really, as opposed to merely formally, subsumed under capital.

> [A]t first, the subjection of labor to capital was only a formal result of the fact that the laborer, instead of working for himself, works for and consequently under the capitalist. By the cooperation of numerous wage-laborers, the sway of capital develops into a requisite for carrying on the labor process itself, into a real requisite of production. That a capitalist should command on the field of production is now as indispensable as that a general should command on the field of battle.[15]

It is crucial to avoid a certain misunderstanding here. The claim is *not* that the necessity for a directing authority which promotes exploitation results from cooperation per se, but rather from cooperation within a *capitalist framework*. Marx is clearly acknowledging the determining influence of capitalist relations of production. On the other hand, Marx does claim that the *specific kind* of cooperation which occurs within capitalism is exploitative and alienating, because to characterize this species of cooperation one must make reference to its specific interactive context:

> [T]he cooperation of wage laborers is entirely the operation of the capital that employs them. Their union into one single productive body and the connection between their individual functions are matters which lie outside of them, in the capital which brings and keeps them together. Hence the connection existing between their various labors confronts them ideally as the plan of the capitalist and practically as his authority, as the power of an alien will who subjects their activity to his aims. If, therefore, the control of the capitalist is in content two-fold in virtue of the two-fold nature of the very production process to be led—which on the one hand is a social labor process for producing use values, on the other, a value-expansion process of capital—then in form that control is despotic.[16]

Marx describes at least two other ways in which the exploitation of labor by capital is not merely formally required by the relations of production but also secured through features of the labor process. The first has to do with division of labor; the second, with machinery. During the manufacturing period of capitalist development there arose a division of labor which assigned each person permanently to one detail job. This division of labor developed the productive capacity of combined or cooperative labor, but it did so at the expense of individual productive capacities. In addition to lowering training costs, this transference of individual knowledge and skill to the "know-how" of the collective working organism increases the dependence of the individual worker on that organism and consequently on its director, the capitalist. The worker's dependence is no longer merely due to the fact that he does not own the means of production; now his very skills do not permit the exercise of his labor power apart from the cooperative labor process controlled by the capitalist:

> While simple cooperation leaves the mode of working by the individual for the most part unchanged, manufacture thoroughly revolutionizes it and seizes the labor power of the individual by its very roots. It convers the laborer into a crippled monstrosity, by forcing his detail dexterity at the expense of a world of productive capabilities and instincts . . . . If, at first, the worker sells his labor power to capital because the material means of producing a commodity fail him, now his very labor power refuses its services unless it has been sold to capital. Its functions can be exercised only in an environment that exists in the workshop of the capitalist after the sale. Rendered incapable by nature to make anything independently, the manufacturing laborer develops productive activity as a mere appendage of the capitalist's workshop.[17]

With the industrial revolution and the replacement of handicraft production by production based on the scientific design and utilization of large-scale machinery and other means of production, this technical subjugation of the worker to the dictates of capital is considerably extended. Science and its material embodiments in the production process are developed and utilized not as the individual laborers' own productive powers but rather in the form of alien powers—the productive powers of capital, of congealed labor which has the power of expanding itself at the expense of living labor. Thus we find the following passage in the *Grundrisse*:

> The science which compels the inanimate limbs of the machinery, by their construction, to operate purposefully, as an automaton, does not exist in the worker's consciousness but rather acts upon him through the machine as an alien power, as the power of the machine itself. The appropriation of living labor by objectified labor—of the power or activity which creates value by value existing for itself—which lies in the concept of capital, is posited in production resting on machinery as the character of the production process itself, including its material elements and material motion.

And in *Capital*:

> It is a common feature of all capitalist production, insofar as it is not only a labor process but also a value-expansion process, that it is not the worker that employs the conditions of labor, but the conditions of labor that employ the worker. But it is only with machinery that this inversion acquires technically a tangible reality. By means of its conversion into an automaton, the instrument of labor confronts the laborer, during the labor process itself, as capital, as dead labor which dominates and pumps dry living labor power. The separation of the intellectual powers of production from the manual labor, and the conversion of those powers into the might of capital over labor, is, as we indicated earlier, finally completed by modern industry erected on the foundation of machinery. The special skill of each individual insignificant factory operative vanishes as an infinitesimal quantity before the science, the gigantic physical forces, and the mass of labor that are embodied in the factory mechanism and, together with that mechanism, constitute the power of the "master."[18]

Once again, it is important to avoid a misunderstanding. Wellmer interprets the passage from the *Grundrisse* as asserting that machinery as such is responsible for alienation:

> Now the determinations of alienated labor appear *in toto* as those of the automated production process itself: no longer as the attributes of capital, insofar as "it is in its way the appropriation of living labor," but above all as "in its physical aspect" it has become mechanized. The "animate monster" in contrast to which "living labor" becomes "a mere live accessory," is the machinery itself as the "technological application of science." ... the fact that the workers do not "combine" but are "combined" no longer appears as characteristic of the capitalist context of relations, but as that of the "automatic system of machinery."[19]

In support of this interpretation, Wellmer quotes another sentence from the *Grundrisse* which occurs a few lines down from the above passage: "the production in enormous mass quantities which is posited with machinery destroys every connection of the product with the direct need of the producer and hence with direct use value."[20] Marx is allegedly asserting that any industrial production, i.e., any production which involves the application of science in the design and utilization of large-scale machinery, is alienating, regardless of whether the relations of production are capitalist or noncapitalist. According to this alleged view, the advantage of socialism over capitalism does not lie in any qualitative change in the labor process but rather in the fact that the appropriation of the means of production by the working class allows a scientific regulation of the production process which would bring about a radical shortening of the (necessarily alienating) working day. Wellmer interprets Marx's remarks in *Capital*[21] that there will always be a realm of necessity and that the realm of freedom lies beyond the sphere of material production as an expression of this view.

Yet in the passages cited Marx is not talking about the necessary features of all industrial production, let alone the necessary existence in all forms of society of a realm of necessity—a sphere of productive activities which are not intrinsically desirable but are performed only for the sake of their consequences. Rather he is describing the necessary realization and expression of a specific social power—the power of capital over labor—in certain specific modifications of industrial production. Just as he was not saying above that cooperation in general is exploitative but was only making that claim for cooperation which takes the form of a value-expansion process, he is not saying here that machinery as such or in general is responsible for alienation; rather he is tracing the alienating character of machinery to the specific social form which industrial production assumes in capitalism. He is saying that machinery, in virtue of the specifically capitalist type of process by which it comes to be designed and employed, and its specific design and employment in the interests of value expansion, is a product of labor which confronts the individual laborers as an alien material power to which they must submit their will.

Two features of the specifically capitalist use of machinery which Marx discusses are the wedding of each worker to one detail job and long working hours which leave little or no time and energy for educational development away from the job. Neither of these features is required by all possible production by machinery. The first is due to the capitalist's incentive to keep wages and thus training costs to a minimum and to maximize the worker's dependence on him.[22] The second is due to the fact that to make a living in capitalism, workers have to perform surplus labor for a capitalist.

Marx also argues that certain systems of machinery within capitalism are so designed as to require work of attendance which could be mechanized (with a saving of total social labor time) but is not, because of the requirements of value expansion: the capitalist is not interested in cutting down on society's living labor requirements but in reducing his costs, and these two are not always equivalent because the labor embodied in the wage is less than the labor performed by the worker. Where production is not tied to the necessity of producing surplus value, this particular work of attendance could be mechanized. Thus Marx says that "in a communistic society there would be a very different scope for the employment of machinery than there can be in a bourgeois society."[23] Incidentally, nowhere so far as I know does Habermas criticize this argument. Yet he denies that "the model of a technologically possible surplus that cannot be used in full measure within a repressively maintained institutional framework (Mark speaks of "fettered" forces of production) is appropriate to state-regulated capitalism."[24] If we assume that he is aware of the argument, then either he must regard it as never having been sound or he believes that it has been rendered unsound by developments in advanced capitalism. In either case one would expect an explicit argument from a Marxist who wants to claim that the productive forces are not fettered in advanced capitalism. Indeed, Marx's claim here would seem to be important for a critical understanding of certain features of assembly-line technology and the use of certain relatively labor-intensive techniques in low-wage areas.

All three of the above features of the specifically capitalist use of machinery help to secure a strict separation of the workers from the scientific knowledge embodied in the machines they tend. It is this separation of the workers from the intellectual powers utilized in production, along with the utilization of those powers by capital in the interests of value expansion, which turns machinery into an alien force to which workers must submit.

Socialist relations of production could transform the productive forces of modern industry into the workers' own productive powers. This transformation, however, would involve certain modifications of industrial production. Without claiming to give a complete list of these modifications, we can nevertheless mention the following partially overlapping ones: shortening of the working day and worker education, job rotation, job enlargement, redesign of certain machine systems and other industrial processes, replacement of despotic by democratic supervision, breakdown of the division of mental and manual labor, and even some alterations in the intellectual division of labor. This last modification is especially important to mention because it is easily overlooked that if Marx is right, then the fact that science is a productive force separate from labor and pressed into the service of capital is in part due to specific aspects of intellectual production within capitalism—aspects which are not merely a function of its separation from manual labor but which have to do with its internal organization. At any rate, the aim of a socialist transformation includes the development of individuals as directly social individuals—

individuals with an immediate interest in the satisfaction of each other's needs. Consequently, contrary to the conclusions Wellmer draws from Marx's theory, neither the fact that industrial production is mass production nor the fact that it is at least in part still *work* in the sense of activity which would not be performed were it not for its consequences would preclude its being, in Marx's sense, self-activity, and hence nonalienated labor. The following passage from the *Grundrisse* is quite relevant in this connection, and it should be read in conjunction with Marx's remarks in *Capital* about the nature-imposed requirement for a realm of necessity:

> It goes without saying, by the way, that direct labor time itself cannot remain in the abstract antithesis to free time in which it appears from the perspective of bourgeois economy. Labor cannot become play, as Fourier would like, although it remains his great contribution to have expressed the suspension [*Aufhebung*] not of distribution, but of the mode of production itself, in a higher form, as the ultimate object. Free time—which is both idle time and time for higher activity—has naturally transformed its possessor into a different subject, and he then enters into the direct production process as this different subject. This process is then both discipline, as regards the human being in the process of becoming; and, at the same time practice [*Ausübung*], experimental science, materially creative and objectifying science, as regards the human being who has become, in whose head exists the accumulated knowledge of society.[25]

It is noteworthy that this passage occurs just nineteen pages after the one which Wellmer interprets as asserting that industrial production is in general alienating, apart from capitalist relations of production.

Habermas and the Real Subsumption

Marx saw it as crucial for an adequate critical theory to recognize the relation between the production process and the value expansion process as one of content to form. He saw this relation as a further development of the relation between the two aspects of commodity-producing labor as on the one hand productive of use values and on the other productive of value. And he called comprehension of this latter relation "the whole secret of the critical conception."[26] Only when the connection between the labor process and capitalist relations of production is viewed in this way can an adequate understanding be achieved of power relations and ideology.

The implications for power relations should by now be fairly clear: The real subsumption of labor under capital is the realization of the capital-labor relation as a specific form of the production process, and consequently the dependency of labor on capital goes deeper than mere wage dependency, the mere lack of ownership of the means of production by the worker. Just as the social character of commodity-producing labor must express itself as a property of the products of that labor, so too must the social relations of capitalist production acquire a material-technical shape: certain features of the production process—e.g., the material subordination of labor to machinery—embody, express, and reproduce the power relations obtaining between capital and labor. Consequently, the replacement of capitalist by socialist relations of production necessarily involves a rationalization of the production process. And this rationalization would not merely consist in a quantitative increase in productive capacity; it would involve a change in the *form* in which productive capacities are developed and utilized. The productive powers of social labor would no longer be developed and utilized in the form of the productive powers of capital and therefore as productive powers extraneous to the individual workers and dominating them; rather, they would be developed and utilized as the workers' own powers.

As far as ideology is concerned, it is precisely the real subsumption of labor under capital which is responsible for the most mystifying aspects of the class relation. The fact that capital must give itself a material-technical shape by expressing itself in the specific design of the labor process is analogous to the fact that the value of one commodity must find expression in terms of the natural features of another commodity (e.g., in ounces of gold). In both cases a social relation of production assumes the form of certain natural properties and processes. In the first case, the consequence is commodity fetishism, the false appearance of value as a natural property of commodities and thus of commodity production as an everlasting (because natural) form of social production. In the second, the consequence is also a type of fetishism: the forces of production (e.g., cooperation, division of labor, machinery, science) appear *as such* to have the power to subjugate living labor.[27] The peculiar exploitation of living labor by dead labor which is capital appears to be due either to certain eternal features of the production process or at least to certain of its features which transcend its capitalist form. It is a basic task of the critique of political economy to counter these mystifications by bringing to light the nature of value and capital as necessarily reified expressions of certain specific social relations of production. The view that industrial production is *per se* alienating falls prey to this reification. It is ironic that Wellmer interprets Marx's account of the real subsumption of labor under capital as an expression of the very sort of view it was formulated to combat.[28]

It is also ironic that Habermas, who wants to retain the ideology-critical features of Marx's theory while discarding its "positivist" framework, is barred by his own conceptual strategy from incorporating the above account of how ideological mystifications function within capitalism. For this account turns essentially on the recognition of certain logical connections between stages in the development of production and interactional contexts, while Habermas is concerned precisely with denying such connections. He is trying to construct a conceptual framework within which production and socialization have logically independent developmental patterns. The critique of political economy cannot be reconstructed within such a conceptual framework without essential loss.

Habermas's claim that technical rationalization and practical rationalization are logically independent, taken strictly, entails that each stage or degree of technical rationalization is conceptually (if not causally) compatible with any stage or degree of practical rationalization. For example, he views an adequate characterization of the incorporation of science into the production process as logically compatible with adequate characterizations of capitalist, socialist, or bureaucratic-elitist relations of production. And for him this stage of technological development is the final stage of technical rationalization. The scientific, technological, educational, and productive apparatus of society, as it has matured within capitalism, is completely rational with respect to the goal of developing productive capacity. To be sure, what capacities are developed, and the uses to which they are put, are not yet tied to democratic decision-making processes, but this is a matter of incomplete *practical* rationalization, not incomplete technical rationalization. It is a matter of wrong *applications of*, rather than *inadequacies in*, our technical reason. All technical questions are now tied to discursive learning processes, and this is the high point of technical rationalization.

But this is not the view of the critique of political economy. It should be clear from the above discussion that while Marx did not attribute alienation to technology in abstraction from social relations of production, it is wrong to express his view as ascribing alienation merely to capitalist property relations and not to technology. The real subsumption of labor under capital involves a technical subjugation of the worker.[29] The state of a society's technology at a given time depends on the range of technically feasible alternative production processes which confront the producers. This range is circumscribed not simply by the existing state of knowledge but more narrowly by the *embodiments* of that knowledge which are actually on hand in the form of developed designs, skills, abilities, and means of production. It was Marx's view that capitalism guided the evolution of these embodiments in a quite specific direction—one which sacrificed certain worker abilities and thereby rendered the worker more dependent on capital. It was also his view that the seizure of political power of the working class would lead to an important change in the direction of this evolution, as we have seen.[30] Marx thus did not believe in the neutrality or political "innocence" of capitalist technology. The transition from capitalism to communism necessarily involves a transformation of technology and not merely a new application of the same technology. Of course, one can always describe technology at a level of abstraction at which it is conceptually compatible with various sets of production relations. At this level, it is a tautology that technology is neutral vis-à-vis the different approaches to practical questions implicit in those different sets of production relations. The real issue is whether at this level of abstraction one can give an adequate characterization of technological development, from the point of view of critical theory. Marx comes down on one side of this issue, and Habermas on the other.

Thus, while Marx clearly distinguishes between the individually crippling division of labor which capital enforces and a qualitatively different division of labor, one which fosters the development of individual talents and the unity of social control and individual control,[31] Habermas seems to view the division of labor as a one-dimensional concept having to do merely with varying degrees of strategic rationality in production. Thus he says that it does not make sense "to go back behind a given level of the division of labor." While Marx wants to *transform* science into labor's own productive force by abolishing the division between mental and manual labor, i.e., by transforming the producer into a scientist qua producer and the scientist into a producer qua scientist, Habermas says, "I don't think we can just demand that scientists should de-differentiate their several roles which they have anyway—that is, as a scientist, as a citizen, as a family member and so on."[32]

The following considerations seem to speak against Habermas's claim that the productive forces are not fettered in advanced capitalism. Society's productive forces are constituted by the abilities individuals have to perform various (possibly coordinated) actions and what objective conditions are in existence which enable these abilities to be utilized. Together these resources—subjective abilities and objective enabling conditions—determine society's productive capacities: what things or states of affairs can be produced, how and with what side-effects, and in what quantity combinations.[33] Evolution of society's productive forces is precisely the evolution of this set of resources. There are many different paths this evolution might take. One path might emphasize the development of resources which allow increased quantity of one or more outputs per unit of one or more inputs. Another might develop resources for improvement in quality of products. One might focus on certain aspects of the production process itself, such as health, safety, enjoyability, possibilities for self-expression, and intellectual activity, while another might show little or no sensitivity to these factors. One path might develop resources allowing sensitivity to ecological balance, while another, through overspecialization and a consequent inability of individuals to understand and take account of ecological ramifications of various actions, might work in the opposite direction.

An adequate characterization of rationalization of the productive forces must be sensitive to the fact that in different historical epochs it becomes important to pursue different paths of development of society's resources. For example, ecological considerations did not have the import in the nineteenth century that they do today. To solve the ecological crisis it will probably be necessary not merely to *apply* existing resources differently but to develop *new* resources, such as the ability to adopt a holistic perspective and various coordinative abilities on the part of all those whose decisions and actions have an effect on the production pattern actually adopted. The difficulties which some contemporary socialist societies are having with ecological problems may in fact be evidence for the claim that the resources necessary for their solution are not yet at hand but are still in the process of being developed.

Once this importance of changing the direction of development is recognized, then the claim that the productive forces are no longer fettered in capitalism appears much less plausible. If a path of development becomes important which cannot be pursued within capitalist relations of production but can be pursued within another set of production relations, then the productive forces are fettered within capitalism. The thesis of the real subsumption of labor under capital asserts that capitalism necessarily pursues a quite specific path of development, one which focuses on resources enabling the reduction of labor time per unit of output (though not maximally, as we have seen) but which manifests indifference to myriad aspects of the production process having to do with the well-being of workers. Marx claimed that from the perspective of the modern working class, this sort of development should be viewed as having been progress because it created conditions which make possible—though only under socialist relations of production—a quite different path of development, one which it is in the workers' interest to pursue, and one which it is objectively important to pursue. To support Habermas's position that capitalism places no fetters on the development of the productive forces one must not only deny the validity of this specific analysis by Marx but must also maintain that capitalism is compatible with whatever paths of development have become feasible and important. One would have to argue, for example, that capitalism could allow both the development of resources necessary to solve the ecological crisis and the development of renewable energy sources. Several recent studies have cast serious doubts on these prospects.[34]

It is worth noting that in taking the position he does on the issue of an adequate characterization of technical rationalization, Habermas is in what he himself regards as bad company. It has been a central goal of the work of the Frankfurt School in general and of Habermas in particular to come to terms with the ideology of technocracy, as exemplified in the view that all remaining social problems are purely technical ones due not to class antagonisms but rather to insufficient advances in science and technology. This view presupposes that stages of scientific and technological development can be adequately individuated apart from their specific interactional (class-relational) contexts. Habermas does not question this presupposition, but rather adopts it himself. He does not question the technocrat's conception of rationality, but merely wants to restrict it to its proper domain. The problem with technocratic consciousness does not lie in its conception of science and technology but rather in its attempts to offer technical solutions to what are essentially practical problems. These problems have a completely different logic; a distinct type of rationality provides criteria of adequacy for their solutions. But if Marx is right, Habermas concedes too much to the technocratic view, because the presupposition he shares with it is false. We have seen how Marx, on the basis of a rejection of this presupposition, develops both a criticism of and an explanation of the origin of views which attribute the alienation identical with capital, a specific class relation, to features of the production process conceived to be independent of this relation. Such views are instances of technocratic consciousness. But Habermas cannot appropriate and develop Marx's criticism of them, so long as he maintains the logical independence of technical and practical rationalization.

Thus it is not surprising to find serious deficiencies in Habermas's recapitulations of the critique of political economy. For example, consider the following rather recent account:

[I]n liberal capitalism the class relationship is institutionalized through the labor market and is thereby depoliticized. Since the source of social wealth—that is, the labor power of the worker—becomes a commodity, and social capital is reproduced under conditions of wage labor, labor and exchange processes take on the double character analyzed by Marx: in producing use values, labor processes serve to produce exchange values. By regulating the allocation of labor power and of goods through the money mechanism, exchange processes serve the formation and self-expansion of capital. The market thereby assumes a double function: on the one hand, it functions as a steering mechanism in the system of social labor, which is controlled through the medium of money; on the other, it institutionalizes a power relation between owners of the means of production and wage laborers. Because the *social power* of the capitalist is institutionalized as an exchange relation in the form of the private labor contract and the siphoning off of privately available surplus value has replaced *political dependency*, the market assumes, together with its cybernetic function, an ideological function. The class relationship can assume the anonymous, unpolitical form of wage dependency. In Marx, therefore, theoretical analysis of the value form has the double task of uncovering both the steering principle of commerce in a market economy and the basic ideology of bourgeois class society. The theory of value serves, at the same time, the functional analysis of the economic system and the critique of ideology of a class domination that can be unmasked, even for the bourgeois consciousness, through the proof that in the labor market equivalents are not exchanged. The market secures for the owners of the means of production the power, sanctioned in civil law, to appropriate surplus value and to use it in a privately autonomous manner.[35]

While it is unreasonable to expect a passage of just a few sentences in length to be an adequate account of the nature and significance of the capitalist process of production as disclosed by Marx's theory, it is important to realize that this passage concerns itself explicitly with an explication of the double character of the production process. From this perspective one can point to a number of inadequacies. For example, Habermas mistakenly refers to the labor power of the worker as "the source of social wealth [*Reichtum*]." Although commodity-producing labor, as abstract labor, is the sole source of *value*, which is a specific social *form* of wealth, labor is not in any society the sole source of *wealth*:

The use values coat, linen, &c., i.e., the bodies of commodities, are combinations of two elements—natural material and labor. If we take away the useful labor expended upon them, a material substratum is always left, which is furnished by nature without the help of man. In production, man can only proceed as nature does, that is, by changing the forms of materials. Nay more, in this work he is constantly supported by natural forces. Thus labor is not the only source of the use values it produces, of material wealth. As William Petty puts it, labor is its father and the earth its mother.[36]

This passage from Marx comes from the section in *Capital* where Marx first discusses the two-fold character of commodity-producing labor. It belongs in that section, because to claim that labor is *the* source of wealth is to confuse wealth with value and thereby to confuse a specific social form of the labor process with labor in general. As we have seen, Marx's analysis of the dual character of the production process is aimed precisely at warding off such confusions.

A similar criticism could be made of the assertion that with the rise of capitalism "social capital is reproduced under conditions of wage labor" and of other passages where Habermas speaks of capitalism as being characterized by a "private form of capital expansion."[37] These passages give the impression that for Habermas capital is a feature of the production process which transcends the specific set of social relations which constitute value in a process of self-expansion. While this use of the term "capital" has been quite common in bourgeois economics, Marx repeatedly criticized it as involving a confusion of specific social with natural forms of production.

The passage also superficially characterizes the class relationship in capitalism merely as wage dependency. As we have seen, the critique of political economy asserts that the dependency of labor on capital goes much deeper than that and is secured in the production process via forms of cooperation and division of labor, and design and use of the means of production. Habermas cannot appropriate this insight because he views production merely as purposive-rational action and thus production in capitalism as not socioeconomically specific to capitalism. This explains the emphasis on the regulating function of market phenomena, whereas for Marx these phenomena, though they do have a role in the regulation of the overall process, are socially necessary indicators of developments in the sphere of production.

Finally, a related inadequacy is the impoverished characterization of Marx's theory as critique of ideology. Habermas refers only to Marx's criticism of the ideology of equivalent exchange. He does not mention the critique of the mystification in virtue of which the forces of production seem to have the character of capital by nature, just as gold seems to be by nature money. This omission is not a peculiarity of this particular passage;

it is typical of Habermas's characterizations of the ideology-critical functions of the critique of political economy.[38] Yet one must insist that the domination of labor by capital *cannot* be unmasked—at least not completely—without a comprehension of the real subsumption of labor under capital and its attendant mystifications.

A Controversial Text

It would not be appropriate to close this chapter without a discussion of the long passage from the *Grundrisse* which we quoted on pp. 70-71 and which Habermas and Wellmer interpret as an important manifestation of Marx's technocratic tendency.[39] The reader will recall that in this passage Marx anticipates that a socialist transformation of society will come about as a result of the development of large-scale industry and the application of science to the production process. Allegedly ignored here is the "dimension of power relations that regulate human beings' interaction among themselves."[40] Marx is allegedly forgetting that what is required to achieve self-conscious control of the social life process by the associated producers is a rationalization of these power relations through a process of reflection which, though it may be prompted by the development of the productive forces, is nevertheless not logically entailed by that development.

A proper understanding of the allegedly technocratic passage can be achieved only by taking into account the context in which it occurs. The fundamental concern of the portion of the *Grundrisse* which contains the passage is to present the contradictory nature of capitalism as a system of wealth production which takes the form of a value-expansion process in such a manner as to make it clear that this contradictory nature, which is latent in the two-fold nature of the commodity as use value and bearer of value, is responsible not only for the growth and development of the capitalist system, but also for its eventual breakdown and replacement by a higher form of social production. Far from being out of step with the critique of political economy, this concern is its fundamental intention. And far from ignoring power relations secured in ideology, Marx is concerned here to show how capital itself, through the development of its contradictory nature to the point of crisis, cracks its own ideological armor.

Now I do not want to maintain that these passages from the *Grundrisse* are the most lucid presentations of Marx's views, or even that they represent his fully developed conception of the nature of capitalism, its crises and transcendence, but only that they do not represent a departure from the ideology-critical tasks of the critique of political economy. It must be kept in mind that these passages are part of a rough draft written primarily for self-clarification rather than publication. Otherwise one might demand too much of them.

Marx gives the three-page section which contains the allegedly technocratic passage the following title: "Contradiction between the foundations of bourgeois production (the *value measure*) and its development. Machines, etc."[41] By explaining how the section is supposed to be an exposition of the nature of this contradiction, we can reveal its sensitivity to the problem of ideology. One side of the contradiction is the "value measure" as the foundation of bourgeois production. What Marx is referring to here is the fact that value-expansion forms the ruling principle in capitalism. Production proceeds smoothly in capitalism only on the condition that workers perform surplus labor which gets congealed into surplus value. Marx claims that this social form of wealth production is justified only on the presupposition that direct labor time—time spent in direct production as opposed to, say, time spent on education and scientific research—is the most important factor in the production of wealth. However, capital itself in its very development—and here is the other side of the contradiction—works to remove this presupposition and thereby render itself obsolete. By developing the productive powers of combined labor and by incorporating science into the production process, capital makes direct labor time an increasingly unimportant factor in the production of wealth compared to the social organization of the production process and the development of science and technology. Furthermore, by tremendously increasing the productivity of labor, it makes possible a significant reduction in direct working time, a reduction which would allow for the optimum utilization of these newly important factors through the development of the entire population as directly associated individuals in self-conscious control of their process of production. Capital, however, is incapable of realizing these possibilities which it creates, because it enforces surplus labor time on the part of the masses as a condition of its existence. Capital thus undermines its own raison d'être.

> Capital itself is the litigant contradiction, in that it presses to reduce labor time to a minimum, while it posits labor time, on the other side, as sole measure and source of wealth . . . . On the one side it thus calls to life all the powers of science and of nature as of social combinations and social intercourse, in order to make the creation of wealth (relatively) independent of the labor time applied to it. On the other side, it wants to measure the gigantic social forces generated in this way against labor time and to confine them within the bounds required to preserve as value the value already created.[42]

Of course, the fact that the resources exist which make possible (within socialist relations of production) the development of the conditions of an emancipated society does not entail that the working class will actually undertake that development. Ideological factors, for example, could prevent them from realizing either that the resources do exist or that they are justified in using them. Yet Marx says:

> As soon as labor in the direct form has ceased to be the great well-spring of wealth, labor time ceases and must cease to be its measure, and hence exchange value [must cease to be the measure] of use value. The *surplus labor of the mass* has ceased to be the condition for the development of general wealth, just as the *non-labor of the few*, for the development of the general powers of the human head. With that, production based on exchange value breaks down, and the direct, material production process is stripped of the form of penury and antagonism.[43]

It is primarily these remarks, I think, which have been responsible for the conclusion that the disputed section is apocryphally insensitive to the problem of ideology and espouses some sort of self-actualizing power to technological possibilities, regardless of interactional context. Yet this conclusion is unwarranted. It depends on a strict separation of the problematic remarks from the surrounding context. The two immediately preceding sentences, though not decisive on the issue by themselves, make reference to changes in consciousness brought about by the development of capitalist industry:

> In this transformation, it is ... the development of the social individual which appears as the great foundation-stone of production and of wealth. The theft of alien labor time, on which the present wealth is based, appears a miserable foundation in face of this new one, created by large-scale industry itself.[44]

More important are remarks in the immediately following section to the effect that the destruction by capital of its justifying presupposition is not something that be kept a secret but rather must manifest itself in social crisis:

> The creation of a large quantity of disposable time apart from necessary labor time ... appears in the stage of capital, as of all earlier ones, as non-labor time, free time for a few. What capital adds is that it increases the surplus labor time of the mass by all the

means of art and science, because its wealth consists directly in the appropriation of surplus labor time; since value [is] directly its purpose, not use value. It is thus, in spite of itself, instrumental in creating the means of social disposable time, in order to reduce labor time for the entire society to a diminishing minimum and thus to free everyone's time for his own development. But its tendency [is] always, on the one side, *to create disposable time, on the other, to convert it into surplus labor.* If it succeeds too well at the first, then it suffers from surplus production, and then necessary labor is interrupted, because *no surplus labor can be realized by capital.* The more this contradiction develops, the more it becomes evident that the growth of the productive forces can no longer be bound up with the appropriation of alien surplus labor, but the mass of workers themselves must appropriate their own surplus labor. Once they have done so—and *disposable time* thereby ceases to have an *antithetical* existence—then on the one hand necessary labor time will be measured by the needs of the social individual, and on the other the development of the power of social production will proceed so rapidly that, even though production is now calculated for the wealth of all, *disposable time* grows for all. For real wealth is the developed productive power of all individuals.[45]

A link is clearly being asserted here between interruptions in the value expansion process, brought on by the development of that process itself, and the formation of an anticapitalist consciousness. The reification of social relations in capitalism makes it appear, when the value expansion process is proceeding smoothly, that the productive forces are inseparable from their form as capital, just as use value seems inseparable from value. But an interruption of the process provides, as Habermas himself says, a "practical critique of ideology."[46] Idle workers and idle machines, people in need amidst a plethora of wealth in the form of unsaleable commodities—this situation makes it apparent, if it does nothing else, that the production and appropriation of wealth are not being hindered by *natural* barriers but by *social* ones.[47]

Another sentence in the controversial section which Habermas and Wellmer cite as evidence for their view, but which they misinterpret, is the following:

The development of fixed capital indicates to what degree general social knowledge has become an immediate force of production, and therefore the conditions of the social life process itself have come under the control of the general intellect.[48]

Marx is allegedly claiming here that democratic control of the social life process has been attained to the degree that fixed capital develops. But this interpretation presupposes that by "control of the general intellect" Marx means control by the associated individual producers. And this reading is completely unwarranted. In *Capital* Marx criticizes Andrew Ure for confusing two distinct descriptions of the capitalist factory system:

> These two descriptions are far from being identical. In one, the collective laborer, or social body of labor, appears as the dominant subject, and the mechanical automaton as the object; in the other, the automaton itself is the subject, and the workers are merely conscious organs, coordinated to its unconscious organs and together with them subordinated to the central moving power. The first description is applicable to every possible employment of machinery on a large scale, the second is characteristic of its use by capital, and therefore of the modern factory system.[49]

In the sentence from the *Grundrisse* Marx is simply describing the utilization of science by the "collective laborer," which is indicated by the development of fixed capital. Control by the general intellect is, as in the passage from *Capital*, control by this collective laborer. There is no implication that it is also control by the individual producers. In fact, as we have seen, Marx persistently points out that in capitalism individuals are subjugated by the general intellect.

In sum, Marx claims in the portion of the *Grundrisse* under dispute that the development of large-scale industry in the form of a value expansion process engenders the following: (1) conditions of production in which the development of the social individual is the most important factor for the satisfaction of human needs; (2) the resources necessary for pursuing such a process of development; (3) awareness of (1) and (2); and (4) the revelation by capital through self-induced crises that it is an inadequate social form for developing the social individual and that only socialist relations of production can provide an adequate form. Marx also claims that these four conditions will lead to a socialist revolution. Now although the nonoccurrence of socialist revolutions so far in developed capitalist societies does not by itself falsify these claims (because of the somewhat idealized nature of Marx's theoretical model), I do not wish to argue here that these claims are true. In the final analysis, it may turn out that they are false—that even under the idealized conditions assumed by Marx (e.g., the absence of international flows of value and capital) there are certain interactive capacities or forms of social consciousness necessary as preconditions for a socialist transformation which would not be brought into being merely by the development of large-scale industry within capitalist relations of production. Even if the claims are true, it is of crucial importance for Marxists to provide a proper account of the relative lack of success of the socialist movement within developed capitalism. In either case, Habermas's studies on the development of interactive competence are quite relevant and should be taken seriously. Marx's views on the development of class consciousness are certainly incomplete, and they may be incorrect as well—either because of a faulty theory of economic crisis or because of a faulty theory of how the antagonisms of capitalist development lead to the dissolution of ideology. What I wish to claim here is that it is wrong to diagnose this inadequacy as due to a technocratic conception of history which brackets out the development of interactive competence. Of course, if my earlier arguments are correct, Marx sees the development of interactive competence as inextricably bound up with the development of productive competence, but this view does not represent an attempted reduction of historical progress to Habermas's concept of technical rationalization. The concept of productive activity which Marx employs is not Habermas's concept of purposive-rational action but is rather one of a process which has social or communicative interaction as a "moment" or aspect. The rationalization which he envisages for this process clearly encompasses the formation of a socially operative self-conception or identity on the part of individuals which is in accordance with their nature as social beings. And this rational identity is not seen as simply entailed by the idea of a production process rendered scientific. Rather, capital's specific utilization of science is seen as both creating resources enabling the development of such an identity and pointing the way toward such a development.

NOTES

1. *Knowledge and Human Interests*, p. 53.
2. Ibid., p. 51.
3. Ibid., p. 62.
4. Ibid., p. 53.
5. The idea of reduction sketched here is similar to Gustav Bergmann's explications of the concept. See his "Reduction," in *Current Trends in Psychology and the Behavioral Sciences* (Pittsburgh: University of Pittsburgh Press, 1954), and Ch. 3 of his *Philosophy of Science* (Madison: University of Wisconsin Press, 1957).
6. *Knowledge and Human Interests*, p. 328.
7. *Grundrisse*, p. 96.

8. *Zur Rekonstruktion,* pp. 145-6; "Towards a reconstruction of historical materialism," pp. 287-8.

9. Especially interesting in connection with the arguments of this chapter are pp. 304-12 of the *Grundrisse,* where Marx is working out some aspects of his treatment of the production process as the content of capital.

10. G.W.F. Hegel, *The Logic of Hegel,* trans. from his *The Encylopedia of the Philosophical Sciences* by William Wallace (2d ed., rev.; London: Oxford University Press, 1892), pp. 242-4 (par. 133). See also W.T. Stace, *The Philosophy of Hegel* (New York: Dover, 1955), pp. 201-202.

11. A detailed discussion by Marx of the difference between the formal and the real subsumption of labor under capital is to be found in his *Resultate des unmittelbaren Produktionsprozesses* (Frankfurt: Verlag Neue Kritik, 1974), pp. 45-84. See also *Capital,* I, pp. 509-11.

12. Surplus labor time is the time devoted to surplus value production, while necessary labor time is the time devoted to reproducing the value of labor power. The production of relative surplus value is discussed by Marx in *Capital,* I, Pt. IV.

13. *Capital,* I, p. 325.

14. Ibid., pp. 330-31.

15. Ibid.

16. Ibid., pp. 331-2.

17. Ibid., pp. 360-1.

18. *Grundrisse,* p. 693; *Capital,* I, p. 423.

19. *Critical Theory of Society,* p. 112.

20. *Grundrisse,* p. 694.

21. *Capital,* III, p. 820.

22. *Capital,* I, p. 422.

23. Ibid., p. 393, n. 1. See also pp. 421-2 of the same volume and pp. 261-2 of Vol. III.

24. *Toward a Rational Society,* p. 119.

25. *Grundrisse,* p. 712.

26. Letter from Marx to Engels of January 8, 1868, in Karl Marx and Friedrich Engels, *Werke,* XXXII (Berlin: Dietz Verlag, 1965), p. 11. In another letter to Engels dated August 24, 1867, Marx said: "The best things in my book are 1. (on this rests all understanding of the facts) the *double character of labor,* stressed immediately in the *first* chapter, according to whether it is expressed in use value or exchange value; 2. the treatment of *surplus value independently of its special forms* as profit, interest, ground rent, etc." (*Werke,* XXXI (1965), p. 326). We have already seen that in the opening chapter of *Capital* itself Marx states that the understanding of the two-fold nature of the labor contained in commodities "is the pivot on which a clear comprehension of political economy turns" (I, p. 41).

27. See *Resultate des unmittelbaren Productionsprozesses,* pp. 77-84; *Capital,* III, 826-7; *Theories of Surplus Value,* Pt. III, pp. 389-92.

28. Possible Marxist responses to the view that industrial production per se is alienating are discussed and appraised in a paper by Bernard Gendron and Nancy Holmstrom, "Marx, machinery, and alienation," in *Research in Philosophy and Technology* III (JAI Press, forthcoming).

29. This is recognized by Göran Therborn, "Jürgen Habermas: a new eclecticism," *New Left Review* 67 (May-June 1971): 76, n. 14.

30. See also *Capital,* I, pp. 486-8.

31. Ibid., pp. 364-6 and 488.

32. "Habermas talking," p. 46.

33. I know of no reason to exclude communicative competence from this set of resources, since the type and level of such competence affects what can be produced and thus what needs can be satisfied.

34. See, for example, two books by Barry Commoner: *The Closing Circle* (New York: Alfred A. Knopf, 1971); and *The Poverty of Power* (New York: Alfred A. Knopf, 1976).

35. *Legitimation Crisis*, pp. 25-6; *Legitimationsprobleme im Spätkapitalismus*, pp. 42-3.

36. *Capital*, I, p. 43.

37. *Toward a Rational Society*, pp. 105, 112; *Technik und Wissenschaft als "Ideologie"*, pp. 80, 90.

38. In Ch. 3 of *Knowledge and Human Interests*, Habermas connects the ideology of equivalent exchange with commodity fetishism in an erroneous way. He says that the "institution of the free labor contract . . . congeals productive activity into the commodity form" (p. 59), and he consequently sees the criticism of the ideology of fair exchange as being executed by Marx's critique of commodity fetishism. Wolfgang Müller has pointed out the mistake here: the commodity form of the products of labor, thus the existence of value as congealed productive activity, and thus commodity fetishism existed before labor power itself became a commodity. The section on the fetish character of commodities in the opening chapter of *Capital* does not yet bring in consideration of class antagonism and its concealment by the ideology of fair exchange (Wolfgang Müller, "Habermas und die 'Anwendbarkeit' der Arbeitswerttheorie," *Socialistische Politik*, 1. Jahrgang, Nr. 1 (April 1969): p.44, n.33.

39. *Grundrisse*, pp. 704-6.

40. *Knowledge and Human Interests*, p. 51.

41. *Grundrisse*, p. 704.

42. Ibid., p. 706.

43. Ibid., pp. 705-6.

44. Ibid., p. 705.

45. Ibid., p. 708.

46. *Legitimation Crisis*, p. 29.

47. In another connection Lukács expresses the relation asserted here between the intensification of the contradictions of capitalism and the breakdown of ideology: "On closer examination the structure of a crisis is seen to be no more than a heightening of the degree and intensity of the daily life of bourgeois society. In its unthinking, mundane reality *that* life seems firmly held together by 'natural laws'; yet it can experience a sudden dislocation because the bonds uniting its various elements and partial systems are a chance affair even at their most normal. So that the pretense that society is regulated by 'eternal, iron' laws which branch off into the different speical laws applying to particular areas is finally revealed for what it is: a pretense" (Georg Lukács, *History and Class Consciousness*, trans. by Rodney Livingstone (Cambridge, Mass.: MIT Press, 1971), p. 101.)

48. *Grundrisse*, p. 706.

49. *Capital*, I, p. 419.

Chapter 7

THE FALLING RATE OF PROFIT

Habermas claims that the Marxian theory that the profit rate has a tendency to fall was true of liberal capitalism but is not true of advanced capitalism. The reason he gives for this change is that scientific and technological progress, which by increasing productivity works against the downward pressure on the rate of profit, was fortuitous in liberal capitalism and thus could have only a limited effect, whereas it has been institutionalized in advanced capitalism and therefore now places systematic emphasis on influences working against declining profitability.[1] In the present chapter it is argued that this criticism makes use of a mistaken notion of the desired status of the law of the tendential fall of the profit rate within the Marxian theory of capitalist development. Marx thought he had located in the law a barrier to the process of capital accumulation which would eventually arise *regardless* of the rate of technological progress, and indeed in some sense *because* of increasing productivity:

> The rate of profit does not fall because labor becomes less productive, but because it becomes more productive. Both the rise in the rate of surplus value and the fall in the rate of profit are but specific forms through which growing productivity of labor is expressed under capitalism.[2]

If this hypothesis by Marx is correct, then the institutional fusion of scientific and technological development cannot invalidate the law in the manner Habermas suggests. Whether or not it is correct is the central question examined in this chapter. A definitive answer is not reached, although some progress is made.[3]

Marx and Habermas on the Dynamics of Capital Accumulation

According to Marx, capital has an immanent barrier, i.e., it is a system of social relations which must break down because of its internal structure. It is like an organism whose life-span is doomed to be finite because of its genetic make up, i.e., regardless of environmental conditions. To be sure, the course of any actual crisis is to be explained by reference to external as well as internal factors, just as the actual development of an organism is to be explained by reference to interaction between genes and environment. The food supply made available to an organism by its environment affects its actual course of development; similarly, weather conditions affect the productivity of labor in agriculture and hence the workings of the entire economic system. Marx, however, did not wish to rely on such extrasystemic considerations when he asserted the inevitable breakdown of capitalism. According to him "the real barrier to capital is capital itself";[4] the historical transitoriness of the capitalist mode of production is necessitated by contradictions in its internal structure.

Marx saw the tendency of the rate of profit to fall as just such an immanent barrier. He repeatedly criticized attempts to explain this tendency by reference to factors external to capital. For example, Ricardo's explanation referred to decreasing productivity in agriculture due to cultivation of less fertile lands in the course of capital accumulation. With regard to this explanation, Marx said of Ricardo: "He flees from economics to seek refuge in organic chemistry."[5] Though Marx on one occasion reverted to a Ricardian type of argument himself,[6] his central aim was to demonstrate a falling tendency of the rate of profit which was rooted not in environmental insufficiency but in factors internal to the capital relation itself.

In evaluating Marx's arguments for the alleged law, then, the primary question should be: How well do they demonstrate an immanent barrier? To show that insufficient profitability is a barrier immanent to capital, it is necessary to show that a decline in profitability would occur even under optimal environmental conditions. Put negatively: the arguments aimed at demonstrating a tendency for the profit rate to fall cannot rely on exogenously determined insufficiencies in the system environment.

Habermas does not approach the question in this way. According to him, the profit rate possessed a tendency to fall in liberal capitalism because scientific and technical progress, which raises the rate of surplus value and cheapens the elements of constant capital, was only sporadic. The dominant pressure on the rate of profit was thus, as Marx said, the downward one provided by an increasing ratio of the value of constant capital (dead labor) to living labor. In advanced capitalism, however, the institutionalization of scientific and technical progress places systematic emphasis on upward pressures on the rate of profit, so that no unambiguous tendency toward declining profitability can be discerned. Regardless of the truth or falsity of these assertions, they reflect a different approach from that of Marx to the question of a tendency of the profit rate to fall, for they assert such a tendency for liberal capitalism only on the basis of environmental insufficiency, viz., a lack of sufficient input of productivity-increasing innovations. They do not assert such a tendency as an immanent barrier.

The fact that Habermas imputes his approach to Marx[7] indicates a misunderstanding of the desired status of the law of the falling tendency of the profit rate in Marx's theory of capitalism. Of course, this misunderstanding is of minor importance compared to the question of the actual dynamics of the profit rate in modern capitalism. A proper understanding and investigation of Marx's approach, however, is of importance in the attempt to answer this question. If Marx's arguments soundly establish the law as a barrier immanent to capital, then under the assumption that capitalism still exists, the institutional changes referred to by Habermas cannot render the law false in the manner he suggests. For Marx's arguments would demonstrate the necessity of an eventual fall in the rate of profit *regardless* of the rate of input of productivity-increasing innovations. The same holds true if Marx's arguments are inadequate but adequate ones along the lines of his approach can be found.

Some of Marx's arguments, such as the one discussed in the next section, are adequate in that they establish part of what he needs to establish concerning the law. His argumentation as a whole, however, is incomplete, and some of his writings on the subject are ambiguous or otherwise not well worked out. What follows is a presentation of some considerations which bear importantly on the issue of whether sound arguments can be found which demonstrate a tendency toward a decline in profitability as a barrier immanent to capital.

The Rate of Surplus Value

Henceforth we shall drop the simplifying assumption made on p. 60 that all components of capital have a turnover period of one year and consequently that the capital advanced is equal to the capital consumed in the course of the year.[8] However, we shall continue for the time being to assume that the annual rate of profit for the society is equal to the surplus value produced during the year divided by the value of the capital advanced for the year's production. That is, we shall assume that the rate of profit r is given by the equation:

$$r = \frac{s}{c^* + v^*} \qquad\qquad [1]$$

where s is the annually produced surplus value and c^* and v^* are the advanced constant and variable capital, respectively. Now a proper treatment of the so-called transformation problem, the problem of the relation between values and prices of production, reveals that this assumption holds only under certain special circumstances.[9] Nevertheless, we shall follow Marx and keep to this assumption in this and the next section in order to bring out clearly the significance of some of his arguments. Later we shall argue that replacing (1) by a more accurate profit determination equation does not invalidate the conclusions we have reached.

If we divide numerator and denominator of (1) by the annual flow of variable capital v, we get the following:

$$r = \frac{\dfrac{s}{v}}{\dfrac{c^*}{v} + \tau} \qquad\qquad [2]$$

where $\tau\ (= v^*/v)$ is the average turnover period for variable capital. It is evident from (2) that increases in the rate of surplus value s/v exert an upward influence on the rate of profit. However, according to Marx, the source of the tendency of the profit rate to fall is a decline in the ratio of the number of workers employed to the value of constant-capital stock.[10] If we assume that such a decline does occur in the course of capital accumulation, then Marx has given a compelling argument for the claim that increases in the rate of surplus value can only retard but not prevent an eventual fall in the rate of profit. The reasoning goes as follows: Since surplus labor time per worker per day has a purely mathematical limit of 24 hours,[11] a point must eventually be reached in the course of capital accumulation when the reduced number of workers employed by a given capital cannot produce as much surplus value as was produced previously by the larger number of workers.[12] Hence the surplus value relative to a given capital, and thus the rate of profit, must eventually fall in the course of capital accumulation.

We may spell this argument out as follows:[13] Since $v + s$ is equal to the annually expended social labor k, and since v and v^* are both nonnegative, the following relationship must hold:

$$r = \frac{s}{c^* + v^*} \leqq \frac{s + v}{c^*} = \frac{k}{c^*} \qquad [3]$$

The rate of profit is bounded by k/c^*. It would attain this upper bound only in the hypothetical case in which $v = 0$, i.e., if workers worked for nothing. In this situation, the total capital advanced would be constant capital and thus equal to c^* in value, and all of the living labor expended would be surplus labor, so that s would equal k.

Now this upper bound, k/c^*, expresses the amount of living labor expended per unit value of constant capital stock. It bears a definite relation to the ratio of the number of workers employed to the value of constant capital stock. If this ratio is given, then k/c^* can be increased only by lengthening the working day.[14] However, such a variation has limits of its own; the length of the working day has an arithmetical maximum of 24 hours and much lower physiological and social limits. Hence we shall assume that the working day is fixed in length at some value. Under this assumption k/c^* is proportional to the number of workers employed relative to the value of constant capital stock.[15] Then it can be seen from (3) that if this number declines in the course of capital accumulation, the concomitant decline in k/c^* will eventually cause a fall in the rate of profit, regardless of possible increases in surplus value per worker due to decreases in v. Hence the increases in the rate of surplus value in the wake of capital accumulation can retard but not prevent a fall in the rate of profit.

Figure 7.1, adopted with minor changes from Okishio,[16] depicts the sort of development indicated by the argument just presented. Fluctuations in the rate of profit due to increases in the rate of surplus value can take place, but the trend is nevertheless downward because of the decreasing upper bound, k/c^*. It should be pointed out that for the argument to

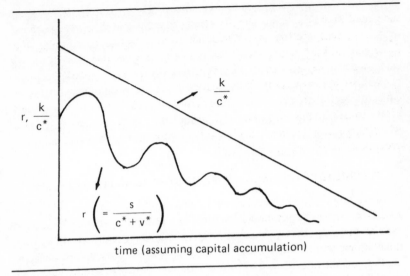

time (assuming capital accumulation)

Figure 7.1

go through, it is not required that capital accumulation entail a continual decline in k/c*, as depicted in the figure, but only a decreasing trend, i.e., a secular decline, one apart from short-term fluctuations. Of course, as has been pointed out,[17] another requirement is necessary, namely that the declining k/c* must not converge upon some positive limiting value. Another way of expressing this requirement is to say that the reciprocal, c*/k, must increase secularly without limit. When we speak of a secular rise in c*/k we shall mean a secular rise so understood.

We may conclude from the foregoing that in one respect at least, Habermas's criticism is misguided. It is not necessary to assume a limited (because fortuitous) input of productivity-increasing innovations in order to derive the dominance of the downward pressure on the rate of profit provided by a decreasing k/c* over the counteracting influence of increases in the rate of surplus value. For such dominance has just been demonstrated under the assumption that the rate of surplus value be allowed to increase without limit.

The Ratio of Dead to Living Labor

According to the above analysis the truth of the law of the tendency of the profit rate to fall hinges on the claim that a secular fall in k/c* is inherent to the capital-accumulation process. Unfortunately, Marx never succeeded in making a sufficiently strong case for this claim. The purpose of the present section is to examine various factors determining the movement of k/c^*, with a view toward ascertaining whether there is such a case to be made. Instead of dealing directly with k/c^*, it will be more convenient to deal with its reciprocal, c^*/k. It is the ratio of the value of constant capital stock to the annual input of social labor, or as we shall prefer to call it, the ratio of dead to living labor. What we want to know is whether a secular increase in this ratio is inherent to the accumulation process.

TECHNICAL CHANGE AND THE RATIO OF DEAD TO LIVING LABOR

According to Marx a secular rise in c^*/k results from technical changes associated with the accumulation process. Ironically, in their desire to expand their capital, capitalists introduce productivity-increasing innovations which work to increase c^*/k, thereby putting a downward pressure on the general rate of profit. In order to evaluate this claim it would be helpful to have a general procedure for determining how various changes in technique—and more specifically ones which increase productivity—would affect c^*/k. The present subsection is devoted to setting up a procedure of this sort.

First we must introduce some additional assumptions and notation:

n — number of different industries or sectors in the economy, each of which produces a single commodity.

a_{ij} $(i,j = 1, \ldots, n)$ — the amount of commodity i *used up* as means of production in the production of a unit of commodity j. The matrix (a_{ij}) is denoted by "A". It tells us the *flow* of constant capital in *physical* terms.

a_{ij}^* $(i,j = 1, \ldots, n)$ — the amount of commodity i *tied up* as means of production in the production of a unit of commodity j. The matrix (a_{ij}^*) is denoted by "A*". It tells us the *stock* of constant capital in *physical* terms.

ℓ_i $(i = 1, \ldots, n)$ — the amount of social labor time directly required for the production of a unit of commodity i. The vector $(\ell_1, \ldots, \ell_n)$ is denoted by "L". It is the vector of direct or living labor inputs.

w_i $(i = 1, \ldots, n)$ — the value of a unit of commodity i, that is, the total labor time (direct plus indirect) socially necessary for the production of a unit of commodity i. The vector $(w_1, \ldots, w_n)$ is denoted by "W". It is determined by the matrix equation

$$W = WA + L$$

which asserts that for each commodity, its value is equal to the value of the means of production used up in its production plus the amount of labor directly expended in its production. Since we shall make the usual assumptions necessary to insure that $(I-A)^{-1}$ exists,[18] we may write

$$W = L(I-A)^{-1}.$$

x_i $(i = 1, \ldots, n)$ the amount of commodity i produced during the year. The column vector

$$\begin{bmatrix} x_1 \\ \cdot \\ \cdot \\ \cdot \\ x_n \end{bmatrix}$$

is denoted by "X". it is the vector of annual gross outputs, in physical terms.

As the reader may have noticed, for the sake of readibility the use of upper-case letters is restricted to denoting matrices and vectors, while lower-case letters (both Roman and Greek) will denote scalar quantities. The elements of a matrix (or vector) denoted by an upper-case letter are denoted by the same letter in lower case with subscripts. For example, the matrix A contains the elements a_{ij} $(i,j = 1, \ldots, n)$, and the row vector L is the vector $(\ell_1, \ldots, \ell_n)$. The identity matrix is denoted by "I," while the zero matrix as well as the zero vector is denoted by "0." The following conventions concerning matrix inequalities are adopted: If A and B are n x n matrices,

$A > B$ means $a_{ij} > b_{ij}$ $(i,j = 1, \ldots, n)$

$A \geq B$ means $a_{ij} \geq b_{ij}$ $(i,j = 1, \ldots, n)$ and for some r,s,

$$a_{rs} > b_{rs}$$

$A \geqq B$ means $a_{ij} \geq b_{ij}$ $(i,j = 1, \ldots, n)$.

A corresponding convention is adopted for vector inequalities.

Now we want to see how technical changes of various sorts affect the ratio c^*/k. The technology employed in the production process is represented, to a certain extent, by the matrices A and A^* and the vector L. Since $c^* = WA^*X$ and $k = LX$, and since $W = L(I-A)^{-1}$, we may relate c^*/k to the technology employed as follows:

$$\frac{c^*}{k} = \frac{WA^*X}{LX} = \frac{L(I-A)^{-1}A^*X}{LX} \qquad [4]$$

Equation (4) expresses c^*/k as a function of the technology employed, as represented by A, A^* and L, and the vector of outputs, X.

As noted above, c^*/k is the ratio of the value of constant capital stock (dead labor) to the amount of social labor expended during the year (living labor) for society as a whole. We have just seen that it depends not only on the technological coefficients a_{ij}^*, a_{ij}, and ℓ_i $(i,j = 1, \ldots ,n)$ but also on the amounts of commodities produced in the various sectors. However, c^*/k is a weighted average of the ratios of dead to living labor in each sector, and these ratios may be expressed solely as functions of the technological variables. To see this we need merely rewrite WA^*X/LX $(= c^*/k)$ as follows:

$$\frac{c^*}{k} = \frac{WA^*X}{LX} = \frac{\dfrac{WA_1^*}{\ell_1}(\ell_1 x_1) + \ldots + \dfrac{WA_n^*}{\ell_n}(\ell_n x_n)}{\ell_1 x_1 + \ldots + \ell_n x_n} \qquad [5]$$

Here A_j^* $(j = 1, \ldots ,n)$ is the jth column vector of the matrix A^*. Thus

$$WA_j^* = \left(\sum_{i=1}^{n} a_{ij}^* w_i \right)$$

is the value of constant capital stock (per unit of output) in sector j and WA_j^*/ℓ_j is the ratio of dead to living labor in sector j. Equation (5) says that the ratio of dead to living labor in the society as a whole is a weighted average of these sectoral ratios, with weights corresponding to the percentages in each sector of the total living labor expended. Since $W = L(I-A)^{-1}$, the sectoral ratios WA_j^*/ℓ_j depend only on the elements of A, A^* and L and not on the output structure.[19]

Since c^*/k is this weighted average of the sectoral ratios and since the weights are all positive, a secular increase in each sectoral ratio or even in the most important[20] sectoral ratios is a sufficient condition for a secular increase in c^*/k. On the other hand, a secular increase without limit of c^*/k is not possible without increases in some of the sectoral ratios. Thus it is an important question how technical change affects the sectoral ratios.

A change in technology may be described by specifying all of the changes which take place in the components of A*, A, and L. Such changes may be represented by a unit vector H defined as follows:

$$H = \alpha(\Delta a^*_{11}, \ldots, \Delta a^*_{n1}, \ldots, \Delta a^*_{1n}, \ldots, \Delta a^*_{nn}, \Delta a_{11}, \ldots, \Delta a_{n1}, \ldots,$$
$$\Delta a_{1n}, \ldots, \Delta a_{nn}, \Delta \ell_1, \ldots, \Delta \ell_n)$$

with $\alpha > 0$ chosen such that $|H| = 1$. H has $2n^2 + n$ components. It might be called the *direction of technical change*.[21]

In order to determine the effect which a technical change of direction H would have on WA^*_j/ℓ_j, the ratio of dead to living labor in sector j, we can find an appropriate expression for $D_H(WA^*_j/\ell_j)$, the directional derivative of that ratio in the direction H. Using the quotient and product rules for differentiation, we first get the following expression:[22]

$$D_H\left(\frac{WA^*_j}{\ell_j}\right) = \frac{\ell_j[D_H(W)A^*_j + WD_H(A^*_j)] - D_H(\ell_j)WA^*_j}{\ell_j^2} \qquad [6]$$

Now we know further[23] that

$$D_H(W) = [WD_H(A) + D_H(L)](I\text{-}A)^{-1} \qquad [7]$$

$$D_H(A^*) = \alpha \Delta A^*, \text{ where } \Delta A^* \text{ is the matrix } (\Delta a^*_{ij}) \qquad [8]$$

$$D_H(A) = \alpha \Delta A, \text{ where } \Delta A \text{ is the matrix } (\Delta a_{ij}) \qquad [9]$$

and $\qquad D_H(L) = \alpha \Delta L, \text{ where } \Delta L = (\Delta \ell_1, \ldots, \Delta \ell_n).$ $\qquad [10]$

Making the appropriate substitutions, we may rewrite (6) as follows:

$$D_H\left(\frac{WA^*_j}{\ell_j}\right) = \frac{\alpha\ell_j[(W\Delta A + \Delta L)(I\text{-}A)^{-1}A^*_j + W\Delta A^*_j] - \alpha\Delta\ell_j WA^*_j}{\ell_j^2}$$

Using the fact that $W = L(I\text{-}A)^{-1}$ and regrouping, we get:

$$D_H\left(\frac{WA^*_j}{\ell_j}\right) = \frac{\alpha}{\ell_j}\left[W[\Delta A(I\text{-}A)^{-1}A^*_j + \Delta A^*_j]\right] \qquad [11]$$

$$+ \left(\Delta L - \frac{\Delta \ell_j}{\ell_j} L \right) (I-A)^{-1} A_j^* \Bigg] \qquad \text{[11 (cont.)]}$$

Equation (11) can give us information concerning the possible effects various sorts of technical change would have on WA_j^*/ℓ_j and thus indirectly on c^*/k. Since the directional derivative of WA_j^*/ℓ_j in the direction H is positive just in case WA_j^*/ℓ_j increases as a consequence of technological change in the direction H, the basic condition which any technological change must satisfy in order to produce an increase in WA_j^*/ℓ_j is that it make the right-hand side of (11) come out positive. If we can determine which changes satisfy this condition, we can then go on to inquire whether such changes are inherent to the accumulation process.

We shall make the following plausible assumptions in order to facilitate determination of the sign of the right-hand side of (11):

A $\geqslant 0$ and in particular each column of A has at least one positive element. [12]

The dominant root of A is less than one (the notion of a dominant root is defined in the Appendix to this chapter). [13]

$L > 0$. [14]

The economic meaning of (12) is that each sector utilizes some means of production; of (13), that positive outputs net of consumed means of production are possible; and of (14), that labor is directly required in every sector. These assumptions allow us to draw the following four conclusions:

$$\frac{\alpha}{\ell_i} > 0$$

$$A_j^* \geqslant 0 \qquad \text{[15]}$$

$$(I-A)^{-1} \geqslant 0$$

$$W > 0.$$

The first of these conclusions follows from (14) and the fact that $\alpha > 0$. Since turnover time is always positive and stocks are equal to flows multiplied by turnover times, (12) guarantees that $A_j^* \geqslant 0$. Assumptions

(12) and (13) guarantee by Theorem II(e) of the Appendix to this chapter that $(I-A)^{-1} \geqq 0$. Since it is known that $(I-A)^{-1}$ is a matrix of total inputs (direct plus indirect) of means of production per unit of output,[24] we may draw the stronger conclusion that not all the elements of the matrix are zero, i.e., that $(I-A)^{-1} \gneqq 0$. In fact, $(I-A)^{-1}$ may have some rows of zeros (the ith row will be zero if the ith commodity is purely a consumption good, i.e., one which is not used as means of production), but each of its columns will have at least one positive element. This last result, along with assumption (14), insures that $W > 0$ since $W = L(I-A)^{-1}$.

Now it is apparent from results (15) and equation (11) that positive elements of ΔA and of ΔA_j^* work to make the directional derivative positive (if they have any effect at all), while negative elements have a negative effect.[25] Thus decreases in turnover time, economy in the employment of constant capital, and "capital-saving innovations," insofar as they express themselves in a decrease in elements of A or A*, will work counter to any tendency which WA_j^*/ℓ_j has to rise.

Let us turn now to a consideration of ΔL, the net influence of which is not so easy to determine. Since $L > 0$, a negative $\Delta \ell_j$ will have an opposite influence on the directional derivative, as the expression "$- \Delta \ell_j/\ell_j$" in (11) would suggest. Indeed, this much can be seen simply from an inspection of the fraction WA_j/ℓ_j, which has ℓ_j in the denominator. Yet negative changes in ℓ_j, and in L generally, also work to lower the values of commodities, and the value vector W occurs as a factor in the numerator. Consequently, such changes will have a negative influence, as can be seen from the position of the expression "ΔL" in (11). Thus changes in L can influence the sign of the directional derivative in both directions, and there is no necessity for these conflicting influences always to cancel each other out or for one always to dominate the other.

In order to get a clearer picture of possible effects of changes in L, we must take a closer look at the column vector $(I-A)^{-1}A_j^*$. We shall assume for the sake of simplicity that the industries which produce means of production form an indecomposable group; i.e., every such industry requires input either directly or indirectly from every other such industry. Since every industry utilizes some means of production, this means that if a row of $(I-A)^{-1}$ has any positive elements, all the elements of that row are positive. This fact, in turn, along with the fact that at least one element of A_j^* is positive, guarantees that $(I-A)^{-1}A_j^* \gneqq 0$. If the ith commodity is utilized at all as means of production, then the ith element of this vector will be positive; otherwise, it will be zero.

Now we may fruitfully discuss three hypothetical technical changes which involve changes in L. The conditions of the first may be stated as follows:

$$\triangle A = 0$$
$$\triangle A_j^* = 0$$
$$\triangle \ell_j < 0$$
$$\triangle \ell_i = 0 \text{ for all } i \neq j$$

Here the only change is a reduction in direct labor inputs in sector j. In this case, referring to (11), we may evaluate the derivative as follows (to simplify the expression we denote the column vector $(I-A)^{-1}A_j^*$ by "G"; it has elements $g_1, \ldots, g_n$):

$$D_H\left(\frac{WA_j^*}{\ell_j}\right) = \frac{\alpha}{\ell_j}\left[0 + \left(\Delta L - \frac{\Delta\ell_j}{\ell_j} L\right)G\right]$$

$$= \frac{\alpha}{\ell_j}\left[\Delta LG - \frac{\Delta\ell_j}{\ell_j} LG\right]$$

$$= \frac{\alpha}{\ell_j}\left[\Delta\ell_j g_j - \frac{\Delta\ell_j}{\ell_j} \sum_i \ell_i g_i\right]$$

$$= \frac{\alpha\Delta\ell_j}{\ell_j}\left[g_j - \frac{1}{\ell_j} \sum_i \ell_i g_i\right]$$

Since $\triangle \ell_j < 0$, if the derivative is nonzero its sign will be the opposite of the sign of the term inside the brackets. This latter sign is in turn the same as the sign of the expression

$$\ell_j g_j - \sum_i \ell_i g_i$$

which is trivially negative or zero,[26] since $\ell_i g_i \geq 0$ for all i. Consequently, $D_H(WA_j^*/\ell_j) \geq 0$ in this case. That is to say, if a reduction in the direct labor input in sector j has any net effect at all on the ratio of dead for living labor in that sector, it will be positive.

The second case concerns the effect of a change in direct-labor input in a sector other than j. The conditions are as follows:

$\triangle A = 0$

$\triangle A_j^* = 0$

$\triangle \ell_k < 0$ where k is some sector different from j

$\triangle \ell_i = 0$ for all $i \neq k$

Under these conditions the derivative may be evaluated as follows:

$$D_H\left(\frac{WA_j^*}{\ell_j}\right) = \frac{\alpha}{\ell_j}\left[\triangle LG - \frac{\triangle \ell_j}{\ell_j} LG\right]$$

$$= \frac{\alpha}{\ell_j}[\triangle LG - 0]$$

$$= \frac{\alpha}{\ell_j}[\triangle \ell_k g_k] \leqq 0$$

Since $\triangle \ell_k < 0$, the derivative in this case is negative or zero, as $g_k \geqq 0$.[27] Thus if a reduction of direct labor input in some sector other than j has any net effect at all, it will be negative.

The third case is one in which a reduction in direct labor requirements takes place in all sectors, and furthermore the rate of reduction is the same in all sectors. Thus

$$\triangle \ell_i < 0 \text{ for all } i;$$

$$\frac{\triangle \ell_i}{\ell_i} = \frac{\triangle \ell_k}{\ell_k} \text{ for all } i \text{ and } k.$$

In this case the net effect of changes in L is zero. The result can be verified as follows: The net influence of L is given by the sign of the term

$$\left[\Delta L - \frac{\Delta \ell_j}{\ell_j} L\right] G.$$

The sign of this term is the same as the sign of the term

$$\frac{\Delta LG}{LG} - \frac{\Delta \ell_j}{\ell_j}. \qquad [16]$$

Now $\Delta LG/LG$ is a weighted average of the terms $\Delta \ell_i/\ell_i$ (i=1, . . . ,n) with nonnegative weights $\ell_i g_i$, as can be seen from the following identity:

$$\frac{\Delta LG}{LG} = \frac{\sum_i \Delta \ell_i g_i}{\sum_i \ell_i g_i} = \frac{\frac{\Delta \ell_1}{\ell_1}(\ell_1 g_1) + \ldots + \frac{\Delta \ell_n}{\ell_n}(\ell_n g_n)}{\ell_1 g_1 + \ldots + \ell_n g_n}.$$

Consequently, since all the $\Delta \ell_i/\ell_i$'s are equal, they are also each equal to the weighted average $\Delta LG/LG$, and thus the value of the term (16) is zero. Hence in this case the changes in L have a net influence of zero.

As stated earlier, Marx saw a secular rise in the ratio of dead to living labor as resulting from technical innovations associated with the accumulation process. These innovations increase productivity, but they do so only by increasing the technical composition of capital, i.e., the means of production, measured in physical terms, employed by a given worker. It is this increase in the technical composition of capital which Marx saw as resulting in a rise in the ratio of dead to living labor.

The foregoing analysis allows us, as we shall see presently, to demonstrate in a rigorous manner that there is no necessary (logical or mathematical) connection either between increases in productivity and increases in the ratio of dead to living labor or between increases in the technical composition of capital and increases in that ratio. One argument in favor of a secular rise in c^*/k is thereby invalidated, namely that of arguing simply from capital accumulation to increasing productivity, from there to an increasing technical composition, and from there to an increasing ratio of dead to living labor. In my opinion, there are reasons independent of the following demonstration for thinking that this strategy is not the most promising to follow, for it seeks to establish the validity of the Marxian law on the basis of growth in productivity per se, i.e., independent of the social form in which it takes place. The arguments of the last chapter concerning the most appropriate method of considering the development of the productive forces would seem to speak here against such a strategy and in favor of an approach which would try to root a secular rise in c^*/k in *particular* methods of increasing productivity which are inherent in the process of capital accumulation. The following arguments, if sound, would provide addtional support for this view.

It is very easy to show that growth in productivity does not necessarily result in an increase in WA_j^*/ℓ_j. By "growth in productivity" here we mean a reduction of the total labor required to produce a given net product. A decrease in any component of the value vector W will bring about such a reduction, provided that it is not accompanied by offsetting increases in other components.[28] Thus if $D_H(W) \leqslant 0$, i.e., if

$$\alpha\,(W \triangle A + \triangle L)\,(I\text{-}A)^{-1} \leqslant 0,$$

then a technical change in direction H is productivity increasing.[29] Thus an increase in productivity can come about as a result of negative changes in the components of A or in the components of L or in both. If we add to the conditions defining the case just discussed (reduction in all components of L at the same rate) the assumption that $\triangle A = 0$, then we have a case of increasing productivity which leaves WA_j^*/ℓ_j unchanged. Another noteworthy case of increasing productivity is the following:

$$\triangle A_j^* = 0$$
$$\triangle A \leqslant 0$$
$$\triangle L = 0$$

This sort of case might obtain as a result of a rationalization of the production process so as to decrease the consumption of some auxiliary material, such as fuel for example. Inspection of equation (11) straightforwardly yields the result that $D_H(WA_j^*/\ell_j) \leqq 0$. Thus no increase is implied in this case.

Marx introduces the notion of the technical composition of capital as follows:

> The composition of capital is to be understood in a two-fold sense. On the side of value, it is determined by the proportion in which it is divided into constant capital or value of the means of production, and variable capital or value of labor power, the sum total of wages. On the side of material, as it functions in the process of production,

all capital is divided into means of production and living labor power. This latter composition is determined by the relation between the mass of the means of production employed, on the one hand, and the mass of labor necessary for their employment, on the other. I call the former the *value composition,* the latter the *technical composition* of capital.[30]

This definition, which refers to means of production *employed* per worker, would seem to indicate that the most appropriate definition, in terms of our notation, of the technical composition of capital in industry j would be the following:

$$T_j^* = \frac{1}{\ell_j} A_j^* = \begin{bmatrix} \dfrac{a_{1j}^*}{\ell_j} \\ . \\ . \\ . \\ \dfrac{a_{nj}^*}{\ell_j} \end{bmatrix}$$

T_j^* is a column vector expressing the proportion of each element of constant capital stock in sector j, in physical terms, to the living labor requirement for that sector. However, in many passages in which Marx discusses increases in the technical composition, it is increases in the *flow* rather than *stock* of means of production per worker to which he refers. These passages would indicate that we should define the technical composition in terms of means of production *consumed* rather than means of production *employed.* We shall not try to choose one definition over the other; rather, we might call T_j^*, defined above, the *stock technical composition* and T_j, defined below, the *flow technical composition:*

$$T_j = \frac{1}{\ell_j} A_j = \begin{bmatrix} \dfrac{a_{1j}}{\ell_j} \\ . \\ . \\ . \\ \dfrac{a_{nj}}{\ell_j} \end{bmatrix}$$

We shall assume that an increase in the technical composition means an increase in both T_j^* and T_j. "Increase" here has the same meaning as for vectors generally. Thus, for example, "$\Delta T_j \geq 0$" means the following:

$$\Delta \left(\frac{a_{ij}}{\ell_j}\right) \geqq 0 \quad (i=1,\dots,n) \text{ and for some } k, \; \Delta\left(\frac{a_{kj}}{\ell_j}\right) > 0.$$

Even under this conception of the technical composition—a conception which is more generous to the position asserting a necessary connection between an increase in the technical composition and an increase in the ratio of dead to living labor than the conception according to which the technical composition must be defined either as T_j or as T_j^* but not both—it can be shown that the alleged necessary connection does not obtain. Consider the following case:

(i) $\Delta A^* = 0$

(ii) $\Delta A \leqslant 0$

(iii) $\Delta L < 0$

(iv) $\dfrac{\Delta\ell_i}{\ell_i} = \dfrac{\Delta\ell_k}{\ell_k} \quad (i,k=1,\dots,n)$

(v) $\dfrac{\Delta\ell_k}{\ell_k} < \dfrac{\Delta a_{ik}}{a_{ik}} \quad (i,k=1,\dots,n)$

Conditions (i) and (iii) entail that $\Delta T_i^* \geqslant 0$, for all i. Conditions (ii), (iii) and (v) entail that $\Delta T_i \geqslant 0$, for all i, since although A and L both decrease the elements of L do so faster than the elements of A. This situation is thus one in which the technical composition of capital increases in all sectors. Yet evaluation of the right-hand side of (11) yields that D_H $(WA_j^*/\ell_j) \leqq 0$. Because of condition (iv), the term

$$\left(\Delta L - \frac{\Delta\ell_j}{\ell_j} L\right)(1-A)^{-1} A_j^*$$

comes out zero (recall the third case discussed above), and the term to which it is added comes out negative or zero, because of conditions (i) and (ii). Hence in this case a rising technical composition does not bring about an increase and may even bring about a decrease in WA_j^*/ℓ_j.

We shall close this subsection with an examination of a case of technological change which will be relevant to the discussion in the next subsection. It is a case in which the technical composition increases in such a manner sufficient to produce an increase in WA_j^*/ℓ_j. The conditions are as follows:

(i) $\Delta A > 0$

(ii) $\Delta A^* > 0$

(iii) $\Delta L < 0$

(iv) $\dfrac{\Delta \ell_i}{\ell_i} = \dfrac{\Delta \ell_k}{\ell_k}$ $(i,k=1,\ldots,n)$

This case might be called one of substitution of means of production for labor, since decreases in L are gained at the expense of increases in A and A^*. That it produces an increase in WA_j^*/ℓ_j is easily seen. Since labor is replaced at the same rate in all sectors (condition (iv)) the net effect of ΔL will be zero, and examination of equation (11) reveals that the effects of ΔA and ΔA^* will be positive.

A RISING RATIO OF DEAD TO LIVING LABOR AS A FUNCTIONAL NECESSITY OF CAPITALISM

Now that we have some idea of what sorts of technical change bring about increases in the ratio of dead to living labor, we need to inquire whether such changes are inherent to the accumulation process. In this subsection we shall consider the claim that a secular rise in c^*/k is inherent to the accumulation process because the alternative—a secularly declining or constant c^*/k—is incompatible with the functional requirements of the capitalist mode of production. The idea here is that a rising c^*/k is the only route open to the capitalist system as a way of avoiding or as a way out of crises of other sorts, such as an interruption in the accumulation process due to an insufficient supply of labor or a realization (underconsumption) crisis in consumption goods industries (Marx's department II). There are expressions of this line of thought in Marx's work,[31] and it has been taken up with varying degrees of sophistication in subsequent discussions.[32] An in-depth exploration of its potentialities is beyond the scope of the present study. We shall instead present one argument of this type in broad outlines and then raise some questions as to its adequacy.

The argument may be stated as follows:

(a) Under conditions of a constant or decreasing c^*/k, the demand for labor power would eventually exceed the supply, thereby putting an upward pressure on wages.

(b) Unless counteracted by a change in the technical composition of capital, which, by raising c^*/k, shifts demand away from labor power toward constant capital, the upward pressure on wages will lead to an interruption of the accumulation process, with crisis-ridden consequences.

(c) Therefore, a crisis resulting from excessive demand for labor power can be avoided only if c^*/k rises.

This argument has a certain degree of plausibility.[33] However, there are two problems associated with using the argument as it stands to support the law of the tendency of the profit rate to fall.

First of all, it is not clear that the argument gives support to the assertion that a *secular* rise is functionally necessary to capitalism. More has to be said to rule out the possibility that periodic rises in c^*/k when the labor supply becomes depleted could prevent crises due to increasing wages and yet be followed by a compensating decline when wages fall, so that there need not be any long-term increasing trend in c^*/k.[34]

Secondly, if we assume that this first problem can be adequately solved, then the argument still does not show that a secular rise in c^*/k is *inherent* to the capital accumulation process, as would be required for the truth of the law of the falling tendency of the profit rate. Provided that the truth of premises (a) and (b) does not depend on some sort of exogenously produced insufficiency in the system environment, then the argument does show, in conjunction with the arguments presented on pp. 128-130 concerning the eventual crisis-producing effects of a secular rise in c^*/k, that capitalism, because of its internal structure, must enter into *some sort* of economic crisis, but not necessarily the sort indicated in the theory of the falling tendency of the rate of profit. In order to vindicate this theory, it would be necessary to show that the threat of crises due to insufficient supply of labor itself *induces* technical changes which result in an increasing c^*/k. Attempts have been made in this direction,[35] but they are as of yet inadequate. It has often been said in this connection that a rise in wages makes profitable and thereby induces substitutions of machinery for labor. There is truth in this assertion. The final case of technological change discussed in the preceding subsection is one in which changes in A^* and A are positive and changes in L are negative. This case is plausibly described as one of substitution of means of production of labor, since reductions in L are gained at the cost of increases in A and A^*. An increase in the wage rate relative to prices of means of production can thus transform a change of this sort from an unprofitable to a profitable venture. And as we saw, this sort of innovation produces a positive change in WA_j^*/ℓ_j. Rising wages thus do bring into play upward pressures on

WA_j^*/ℓ_j. However, certain other technological innovations, as we saw in the last subsection, have a negative effect on WA_j^*/ℓ_j. Furthermore, some of these, such as economy in the employment of constant capital—in general, those which reduce A or A* without involving any positive change in L—remain attractive regardless of increases in the wage rate. There does not seem to be any reason to conclude that the upward pressures on WA_j^*/ℓ_j released by rising wages will necessarily be dominant over the downward influence of these innovations.

It may be, then, that the above argument cannot show that immanent to the capital-accumulation process is the specific barrier of a secularly rising c*/k. Perhaps the most it can show is that even under the most favorable environmental conditions, the capital accumulation process must run into trouble for one or more of a number of different reasons. This, however, would be no small achievement. It would reaffirm the inevitability of economic crises and thereby take much of the sting out of Habermas's criticism of the value-theoretical analysis of capital development, since the main object of that criticism is to show that such crises are no longer a necessary feature of capitalism.

The Transformation Problem

In the foregoing sections we assumed with Marx that the equilibrium rate of profit r is given by the equation

$$r = \frac{s}{c^* + v^*} \qquad [17]$$

and thus that the "maximum" rate of profit r_m—the rate which would obtain if wages were zero—is given by the equation

$$r_m = \frac{k}{c^*}. \qquad [18]$$

A correct solution of the transformation problem reveals that (1) and (2) hold only under certain special circumstances. However, it can be shown that correct equations for r and r_m do not essentially alter the significance of the foregoing analysis. Specifically, the following can be shown:

(i)   A lowering of wages cannot raise the rate of profit above a certain upper bound.

(ii)   The inverse of this upper bound is, like c*/k, a weighted average of the sectoral ratios of dead to living labor. The weights in this average are all nonnegative.

The upshot of these propositions is that as Marx claimed, the sectoral ratios determine an upper bound for the rate of profit, and a secular rise in all of them is sufficient to produce an eventual fall in the rate of profit.[36] Consequently, the preceding investigation retains its relevance.

Before giving proofs of propositions (i) and (ii) we should present a correct set of price and profit determination equations. If we assume that the stock of variable capital is zero, then the equilibrium relative price structure and rate of profit are determined by the following matrix equation:

$$P = P(A + BL) + rPA^*. \qquad [19]$$

Here A, L, r, and A^* are as above, P is the row vector of equilibrium prices $(p_1, \ldots, p_n)$, and B is the column vector

$$\begin{bmatrix} b_1 \\ \cdot \\ \cdot \\ \cdot \\ b_n \end{bmatrix},$$

where b_i is the amount of commodity i received by workers per hour of labor time. B represents the hourly "wage-basket," i.e., the hourly wage rate in physical terms. Thus the column vector $(BL)_j$ of the matrix BL expresses the amounts of each commodity which are consumed by workers per unit output of commodity j. Thus $P(A + BL)$ is the total flow of payments for means of production and labor power per unit of output. Equation (19) says that price is equal to cost of production, $P(A + BL)$, plus the equilibrium rate of profit times total capital invested, rPA^*. If $A + BL$ is nonnegative and indecomposable, and if its dominant root is less than one, then (19) has a positive solution for P, unique up to a scalar multiple, associated with a positive solution for r (this result is based on Theorem I, p. 154). The economic meaning of the indecomposability assumption is that every sector requires input, either directly or indirectly, from every other sector, either as means of production or as a wage good. In making this assumption we are thus abstracting from the existence of any purely luxury sectors. This abstraction is justified, since it can be shown that the conditions of production in such sectors have no bearing on the rate of profit.[37] The economic meaning of the assumption that the dominant root of A + BL is less than one is that positive outputs are possible net of consumed means of production and wage goods.

We may now give proofs for propositions (i) and (ii). The theorems referred to are stated in the Appendix.

Proof of (i): It is known that with a given technology, the rate of profit is inversely related to the wage rate. This can be seen by rewriting (19) as follows:

$$P = P(A + BL + rA^*) \qquad [20]$$

Since A + BL is nonnegative and indecomposable and rA^* is nonnegative, A + BL + rA^* is also a nonnegative, indecomposable matrix. Since $P > 0$, we have from (20) by Theorem I(c) that P is the characteristic row vector associated with the dominant root of the matrix A + BL + rA^*, and this root is equal to one. Since this root is an increasing function of the elements of the matrix (Theorem I(f), reductions in the wage basket B must be compensated for by increases in r in order to keep the root equal to one, if A, L and A^* remain constant. Now, since the root not only cannot drop below one but also cannot exceed one, reductions in B to zero can raise the rate of profit only a certain maximum value r_m, which is given by the equation

$$P = P(A + r_m A^*). \qquad [21]$$

Proof of (ii): We may rewrite (21) as follows:

$$\frac{1}{r_m} P = PA^*(I-A)^{-1}. \qquad [22]$$

Thus $1/r_m$ is the dominant root of $A^*(I-A)^{-1}$. It is also the dominant root of the matrix $(I-A)^{-1}A^*$.[38] Let Z be the nonnegative characteristic column vector of this matrix associated with the root $1/r_m$. Then the following equations holds:

$$(I-A)^{-1}A^*Z = \frac{1}{r_m} Z. \qquad [23]$$

Premultiply each side by the row vector L of direct labor inputs:

$$L(I-A)^{-1}A^*Z = \frac{1}{r_m} LZ. \qquad [24]$$

Then use the fact that $W = L(I-A)^{-1}$ to obtain from (24) the following equation:

$$\frac{1}{r_m} = \frac{WA^*Z}{LZ}.$$ [25]

We have already seen (p. 133) that c^*/k is given by the equation

$$\frac{c^*}{k} = \frac{WA^*X}{LX}.$$ [26]

where X is the column vector of actual annual output. So the difference between $1/r_m$ and c^*/k resolves itself into a difference in the directions of the vectors Z and X. We may rewrite (25) and (26) as follows to reveal that $1/r_m$, like c^*/k, is a weighted average of the sectoral ratios of dead to living labor:

$$\frac{1}{r_m} = \frac{WA^*Z}{LZ} = \frac{\dfrac{WA_1^*}{\ell_1}(\ell_1 z_1) + \ldots + \dfrac{WA_n^*}{\ell_n}(\ell_n z_n)}{\ell_1 z_1 + \ldots + \ell_n z_n};$$ [27]

$$\frac{c^*}{k} = \frac{WA^*X}{LX} = \frac{\dfrac{WA_1^*}{\ell_1}(\ell_1 x_1) + \ldots + \dfrac{WA_n^*}{\ell_n}(\ell_n x_n)}{\ell_1 x_1 + \ldots + \ell_n x_n}.$$ [28]

Since Z is nonnegative, the weights in (27) like those in (28), are nonnegative. Hence a secular increase in each sectoral ratio of dead to living labor is a sufficient condition for a secular increase in $1/r_m$ and thus for a secular decline in the maximum rate of profit. Thus the investigations on pp. 130-145 retain their relevance.

The results of this section, however, do throw some additional light on what sorts of technical change must be inherent in the accumulation process if Marx's hypothesis is to be correct. The maximum rate of profit r_m is the inverse of the dominant root $1/r_m$ of the matrix $A^*(I-A)^{-1}$. Marx's hypothesis thus requires that a secular increase in this root be inherent to the accumulation process. This in turn is not possible without increases in some elements of $A^*(I-A)^{-1}$, since the dominant root is a nondecreasing function of the elements of the matrix (Theorem II(d)).

Now elements of $A*(I-A)^{-1}$ can increase only as a result of increases in elements of $A*$ or $(I-A)^{-1}$; furthermore, elements of $(I-A)^{-1}$, the matrix of total flow requirements of means of production per unit of output, cannot increase without increases in some elements of A, the matrix of direct flow requirements. Hence an increase in $1/r_m$ requires increases in some elements of A or $A*$. And if some elements of A or $A*$ decrease, the increases in others must be even greater than they otherwise would have to be. In this sense the predominant tendency of technical change in capitalism must be toward increases in stocks and/or flows of means of production per unit of output, if the theory of the tendential fall in the rate of profit is to be correct.

A perhaps surprising consequence is that decreases in direct labor requirements have no direct effect at all in lowering the maximum rate of profit. They can have an indirect effect by being cost-reducing factors in technical changes which involve increases in $A*$ or A, thereby making such changes economically attractive. But the maximum rate of profit is not itself altered by changes in the vector L of direct labor requirements, but only by changes in A and $A*$. This conclusion, which was suggested by our earlier analysis of the effects of reductions in L, is a straightforward consequence of the fact that the maximum rate of profit is the dominant root of $A*(I-A)^{-1}$.

Real Wages and the Rate of Profit

In Volume III of *Capital* Marx offers the following account of the incentive a capitalist has to introduce techniques which work ultimately to his disadvantage by lowering the general rate of profit:

No capitalist ever voluntarily introduces a new method of production, no matter how much more productive it may be, and how much it may increase the rate of surplus value, so long as it reduces the rate of profit. Yet every such new method of production cheapens the commodities. Hence, the capitalist sells them originally above their prices of production, or perhaps, above their value.[39] He pockets the difference between their costs of production and the market-prices of the same commodities produced at higher costs of production. He can do this, because the average labor-time required socially for the production of these latter commodities is higher than the labor time required for the new methods of production. His method of production stands above the social average. But competition makes it general and subject to the general law. There follows a fall in the rate of profit—perhaps first in this sphere of production, and eventually it achieves a balance with the rest—which is, therefore, wholly independent of the will of the capitalist.[40]

Our discussion would not be adequate without consideration of an objection to this account by Okishio.[41] He argues that the following proposition holds:

> If a new technology would generate extra profits to an individual capitalist at prevailing prices of production, then the effect of a general introduction of this technology will be to raise the equilibrium rate of profit, provided that the real-wage rate remains constant.

Okishio is working with a simpler model than we are using, but it can be shown that the proposition holds in our model also. We shall first provide such a demonstration and then attempt to assess its significance.[42]

As we saw in the last section, the equilibrium price and profit structure (P,r) with technology (A,L,A*) and real wage bundle B is determined by the following equation:

$$P = P(A + BL + rA^*). \qquad [29]$$

Here P is strictly positive and is therefore the characteristic row vector associated with the dominant root of $A + BL + rA^*$, and this root is equal to one.

The condition for generating extra profits at the prevailing prices with a new technology $(A', L', A^{*\prime})$ is

$$P \geqslant P(A' + BL' + rA^{*\prime}). \qquad [30]$$

Let "M(30)" denote the matrix $A' + BL' + rA^{*\prime}$ which appears in this inequality, and let $\lambda(30)$ be its dominant root. Since $P > 0$, it follows from (30) by Theorem I(g) of the Appendix that $\lambda(30) < 1$.

The new equilibrium price and profit structure (P', r'), consequent upon a generalized introduction of the new technology and with real wage bundle B', is given by

$$P' = P'(A' + B'L' + r'A^{*\prime}) \qquad [31]$$

Let "M(31)" denote the matrix $A' + B'L' + r'A*'$ which appears in this equation, and let $\lambda(31)$ be its dominant root. We know from the equation that $\lambda(31) = 1$.

Since $\lambda(30) < 1$ and $\lambda(31) = 1$, we have that $\lambda(30) < \lambda(31)$. Now if the wage bundle does not change, i.e., $B' = B$, then the only difference between M(30) and M(31) is that the elements of $A*'$ in the latter are multiplied by r' instead of r. Since the dominant root of a nonnegative, indecomposable matrix is an increasing function of the elements of the matrix, the fact that $\lambda(30) < \lambda(31)$ must be due to the fact that $r < r'$, i.e., to the fact that the equilibrium rate of profit has increased. To avoid this consequence requires that some elements of B' exceed the corresponding elements of B, i.e., that there be increases in components of the real-wage bundle.

What are we to make of Okishio's proposition? First of all, it should be noted that it does not contradict the above quoted passage by Marx, since the latter contains no explicit assumption concerning changes in the real wage rate. Yet Okishio's argument is a genuine contribution to the debate, because it shows that the account given in the passage is viable only if it can be shown that technologies which capitalists introduce in order to acquire extra profits at prevailing prices of production tend to induce increases in the real wage rate. Marx does not seem to recognize the necessity for demonstrating such a tendency.

On the other hand, as Mage points out,[43] though Marx never declares explicitly that real wages must tend to rise in the course of capitalist development, this position has a strong implicit basis in his theory: First, Marx asserts that the laborers' "necessary wants" depend on the "degree of civilization" of a society, which he regards as increasing with the development of capitalism. Second, Marx saw modern industry as necessitating an increasing level of worker education (on pain of severe social instability).[44] And third, he regarded increasing intensity of labor as inherent to the process of capital accumulation and as inducing struggles for wage increases to compensate for the increased wear and tear on labor power which accompanies higher intensity:

By increasing the *intensity* of labor, a man may be made to expend as much vital force in one hour as he formerly did in two. In checking this tendency of capital, by struggling for a rise in wages corresponding to the rising intensity of labor, the working man only resists the depreciation of his labor and the deterioration of his race.[45]

In fact, it is plausible that Marx saw the same sort of reciprocal reinforcement taking place between technical change and struggles for wage increases as he did between technical change and struggles for shortening the working day:

> There cannot be the slightest doubt that the tendency that urges capital, so soon as a prolongation of the hours of labor is once for all forbidden, to compensate itself, by a systematic heightening of the intensity of labor, and to convert every improvement in machinery into a more perfect means of exhausing the workman, must soon lead to a state of things in which a reduction of the hours of labor will again be inevitable.[46]

There is also a response on a different level which should be made to Okishio's objection. Though Marx does refer to the desire to make extra profits at prevailing equilibrium prices as a factor in capitalist motivation to introduce new productive techniques, it is not according to him the only factor. We have already referred to suggestions in his work that an upward fluctuation in the money wage level can induce the sort of technical change that puts a downward pressure on the rate of profit. More generally, the threat of worker militancy can provide a strong inducement to technical change. "It would be possible to write quite a history of the inventions, made since 1830, for the sole purpose of supplying capital with weapons against the revolt of the working class."[47] Because capitalist production is an antagonistic process, it is important from the point of view of capital accumulation to develop and utilize techniques which are relatively immune to the threat of worker noncompliance.[48] It seems plausible that the technical changes called for in this regard tend to involve increased use of means of production at the expense of labor and therefore put downward pressure on the rate of profit. The upshot of these remarks is that the process of inducement of technical change in capitalism is more complex than indicated simply by Okishio's criterion of extra profits at prevailing equilibrium prices. Satisfaction of this criterion is probably not even a necessary condition for the introduction of a new technique, much less a sufficient one.

Conclusion

The results achieved in this chapter are sufficient neither for a definitive evaluation of Marx's law of the tendency of the profit rate to fall nor for a complete appraisal of Habermas's critique of it. The key proposition relied upon in the attempt to come to terms with Habermas's views is that if, as Marx thought, the falling tendency of the rate of profit is a barrier immanent to the process of capital accumulation, then Habermas's claim that this tendency has been eliminated in advanced capitalism is false. This conditional proposition was defended, and the remainder of the chapter was devoted to ascertaining the plausibility of its antecedent.

An argument was presented in favor of the claim that increases in the rate of surplus value, no matter how great, can have only a limited effect in counteracting the downward pressure on the rate of profit produced by a secularly rising ratio of dead to living labor. This argument is present in Marx's work. It is not alluded to by Habermas. Yet if it is sound, then contrary to his opinion, the institutionalization of scientific and technical progress cannot vitiate the Marxian law through its effects on the rate of surplus value.

The other proposition necessary to give the law its desired status, namely the proposition that a secular increase in the ratio of dead to living labor is inherent to the process of capital accumulation, is not so well supported by Marx and indeed, if true, is much more difficult to establish. We saw that an increase in the crucial ratio could not be deduced simply from increasing productivity, or even from an increasing technical composition of capital. What is required is an increasing amount of "roundaboutness" in production, in the sense of increases in stocks and/or flows of means of production per unit of output. If Marx's law is true, then it is because capitalism favors this type of technical change over others. Changes of this sort can indeed be induced by wage increases and by various implicit or explicit threats of noncompliance with the dictates of capital on the part of the working class. And these inducing mechanisms do seem to be inherent in capitalist development. These reflections lend plausibility to Marx's law by pointing out that in addition to the general incentive in capitalism to economize on all factors of production there are specific incentives favoring reduction of labor inputs at the expense of increased means of production requirements. Yet these remarks are not sufficient to justify the conclusion that this crucial type of technical change will necessarily dominate other types which increase the ratio of dead to living labor. As we indicated earlier, perhaps the most that can be shown is that the absence of a secular increase in the ratio of dead to living labor itself has crisis-ridden consequences. However, such a demonstration would be quite significant as a reaffirmation of the inevitability of economic crises in capitalism and would therefore run counter to some of Habermas's central claims.

Appendix

We state here without proof some results about nonnegative square matrices which are appealed to in this chapter. These results are commonly used in the study of linear models in economics, and proofs may be found in a number of places.[49]

The n x n matrix A (n $\geq$ 2) is said to be *indecomposable* if no permutation of the rows and columns of A yields a matrix of the form

$$\begin{pmatrix} A_{11} & A_{12} \\ 0 & A_{22} \end{pmatrix}$$

where A_{11} and A_{22} are square.

Theorem I. If A $\geq$ 0 is an indecomposable square matrix, then:
(a) A has a characteristic root $r^* > 0$ such that
(b) to r^* can be associated a characteristic vector $X^* > 0$
(c) there is no nonnegative characteristic vector other than X^*
(d) if r is any characteristic root of A, then $|r| \leq r^*$
(e) for all $s > r^*$, sI-A is nonsingular and $(sI-A)^{-1} > 0$
(f) r^* is an increasing function of every element of A
(g) for any vector X $\geq$ 0 and any s, if AX $\leq$ sX, then $r^* < s$.

If we do not require A to be indecomposable, then we can get the following results:

Theorem II. Let A $\geq$ 0 be an n x n matrix. Then:
(a) A has a characteristic root $r^* > 0$ such that
(b) to r^* can be associated a characteristic vector $X^* \geq 0$
(c) if r is any characteristic root of A, then $|r| \leq r^*$
(d) r^* is a nondecreasing function of every element of A
(e) for all $s > r^*$, sI-A is nonsingular and $(sI-A)^{-1} \geq 0$.

The root r^* of the above theorems is often called the *dominant* root of the matrix A.

NOTES

1. See Ch. 4, pp. 59-62 for a more detailed explication of Habermas' position.
2. *Capital*, III, p. 240.
3. In addition to those acknowledged elsewhere I wish to thank Philip Mirowski, Charles Webster, and Thomas Weisskopf for helpful discussion of issues raised in this chapter.
4. *Capital*, III, p. 250.
5. *Grundrisse*, p. 754.
6. *Theories of Surplus Value*, Pt. III, p. 368. For a recent discussion of this point, see Bertram Schefold, "Different forms of technical progress," *Economic Journal* LXXXVI (December 1976): 806-819.
7. See *Legitimation Crisis*, p. 56.
8. Our model thus incorporates the existence of fixed capital, though perhaps not in the most adequate way, since we do not treat fixed capital as a special case of joint production. The model we use is close to the one presented in Sec. 1.2 of András Bródy, *Proportions, Prices and Planning*, (Budapest: Académiai Kiadó, 1970; Amsterdam and London: North Holland, 1970; New York: American Elsevier, 1970).
9. There is a good discussion of the transformation problem in Alfredo Medio's "Profits and surplus-value: appearance and reality in capitalist production," in *A Critique of Economic Theory*, ed. by E. K. Hunt and Jesse G. Schwartz (Baltimore: Penguin, 1972). For a recent criticism of Marx's approach to the transformation problem, see Ian Steedman, *Marx after Sraffa* (London: New Left Books, 1977).
10. See Ch. 4, pp. 59-60 for a presentation of the basic elements of Marx's view.
11. Here we abstract from possible nonuniform changes in the intensity or in the productivity of labor; such changes make it possible for a worker to perform more than one hour's social labor in an hour (see *Capital*, I, pp. 318 and 524-5). Similarly, it is assumed throughout that we are dealing with simple (unskilled) labor.
12. See *Capital*, III, p. 247.
13. I am indebted in part to Nobuo Okishio, "Technical changes and the rate of profit," *Kobe University Economic Review* VII (1961): 89-90, for the following way of presenting the matter.
14. An unstated assumption here is that the number of working days in the year is constant. If m is the average number of employed workers in the society, y the length of the working day, and z the number of working days in the year, then

$$k = myz.$$

Dividing both sides by c^*, we get that

$$\frac{k}{c^*} = \frac{m}{c^*} yz.$$

This equation relates k/c^* to m/c^*, the ratio of workers employed to value of constant capital stock. It reveals that under the assumption that z is constant, the only way for k/c^* to increase while m/c^* does not is through an increase in y. It can also be seen that if both y and z are constant, then k/c^* is proportional to m/c^*.

15. See n. 14.

16. Okishio, "Technical changes and the rate of profit," p. 89.

17. Heinz Holländer, "Das Gesetz des tendenziellen Falls der Profitrate," *Mehrwert* 6 (June 1974): 114n.

18. It turns out that the conditions on A imposed by the need to have a viable production system, i.e., one which is minimally in a self-replacing state, guarantee that I-A has an inverse. See, for example, Bródy, *Proportions, Prices and Planning,* Sec. 1.1, especially pp. 24-5, and Appendix II. A slightly different treatment is given by Michio Morishima, *Marx's Economics* (New York and London: Cambridge University Press, 1973), Chs. 1 and 2.

19. Some authors have called WA_j^*/ℓ_j the organic composition of capital in sector j and c^*/k the organic composition of the total social capital (e.g., Shane Mage, *The Law of the Falling Tendency of the Rate of Profit* (Ph.D. dissertation, Columbia University, 1963), pp. 68-74; Okishio, "Technical changes and the rate of profit," p. 89; Geoff Hodgson, "The theory of the falling rate of profit," *New Left Review* 84 (March-April 1974): 60, 80-81; and Milton Fisk, "Rate of profit and class struggle," *Radical Philosophers' News Journal* 5 (August 1975): 3). This practice is better than simply identifying the organic composition and the value composition, as does Joseph Gillman, *The Falling Rate of Profit* (London: Dennis Dobson, 1957), p. 16. Yet we have refrained from this practice because while c^*/k may do much of the work which Marx wanted the organic composition of capital to do, he nevertheless defines the organic composition differently. He says: "I call the value composition of capital, insofar as it is determined by its technical composition and mirrors the changes of the latter, the *organic composition* of capital" (*Capital,* I, p. 612). Fortunately, for purposes of the present discussion we do not have to try to unpack this statement. For further discussion of the concept of the organic composition of capital see Holländer, "Das Gesetz," pp. 110-12; Veit-Michael Bader et al., *Krise und Kapitalismus bei Marx* (2 vols., n.p.: Europäische Verlagsanstalt, 1975), I, pp. 190-98; and Steedman, *Marx after Sraffa,* pp. 132-6.

20. Importance here is determined by the relative amount of the year's social labor which is expended in the sector.

21. By "technical change" here we mean a change in the prevailing techniques actually employed in the production process, regardless of whether the new technique represents an increase in the stock of productive knowledge. It should also be pointed out that the model being constructed here may not be adequate to represent certain kinds of technical change so understood. I am thinking here of the fact that changes in A, A*, and L over time are not merely quantitative. New commodities are invented and produced, and old ones are dropped from production.

22. If M is the matrix (m_{ij}), then $D_H(M)$ is the matrix $(D_H(m_{ij}))$. Similarly for vectors.

23. Equation (7) may be derived as follows:

$$W = WA + L$$
$$D_H(W) = D_H(W)\,A + W\,D_H(A) + D_H(L)$$
$$D_H(W)\,(I\text{-}A) = W\,D_H(A) + D_H(L)$$
$$D_H(W) = [W\,D_H(A) + D_H(L)]\,(I\text{-}A)^{-1}. \tag{7}$$

Equations (8) – (10) are applications of the theorem in calculus that the directional derivative of a function f at a point P in the direction H is the dot product of the gradient of f at P and the vector H. See, for example, Robert Creighton Buck and Ellen F. Buck, *Advanced Calculus* (New York: McGraw-Hill, 1965), p. 397.

24. Kelvin Lancaster, *Mathematical Economics* (New York: Macmillan, 1968), pp. 85-6.

25. It should also be noted that for any $i \neq j$, ΔA^*_i does not necessarily induce any change in WA^*_j/ℓ_j, as can be seen from (11). This is to be expected because the vector of commodity values is not definitionally a function of the matrix of constant capital stock, A^*, but only of A and L.

26. The zero case would occur only if j is the only commodity used as means of production. Then for any $i \neq j$, $\ell_i g_i = 0$.

27. The zero case here occurs when commodity k is purely a consumption good, i.e., not used at all as means of production.

28. If X is the vector of gross outputs, the net product Y is equal to the gross product minus the consumed means of production:

$$Y = X - AX.$$

The value of the net product, WY, is thus given by the following equation:

$$WY = W(X-AX) = W(I-A)X.$$

Since $W = L(I-A)^{-1}$, we have

$$WY = L(I-A)^{-1}(I-A)X = LX.$$

The value of the net product is thus equal to the total labor time expended during the year. Consequently, a reduction in any component of W will reduce total labor requirements for a given net output Y. I am indebted to Thorsteinn Vilhjálmsson for noticing an error in an earlier formulation of this argument.

29. That $D_H(W) = \alpha(W\Delta A + \Delta L)(I-A)^{-1}$ follows from equations (7), (9), and (10).

30. *Capital*, I, p. 612.

31. *Capital*, I, Ch. XXV, Secs. 1 and 2; *Capital*, III, Ch. XV.

32. For example, the strategy is explicitly undertaken by Bader and his collaborators in *Krise and Kapitalismus bei Marx*, I, pp. 190-236; see especially pp. 198-201. See also Vol. II of the same work, pp. 387-477.

33. Support for both premises can be found in *Capital*, I, Ch. XXV, Sec. 1.

34. This point is made by Hodgson, "The theory of the falling rate of profit," p. 64.

35. For example, see Mage, *The Law*, pp. 154-157.

36. Okishio also reaches these conclusions for his model in "Technical changes and the rate of profit," Sec. VI and Appendix III.

37. See, for example, Medio, "Profits and surplus value," pp. 340-341, and Okishio, "Technical changes and the rate of profit," Sec. VII and Appendix IV. Marx appears to have been mistaken on this point.

38. The second matrix is obtainable from the first by premultiplying by $(I-A)^{-1}$ and postmultiplying by $(I-A)$. Such transformations leave characteristic roots unaltered. See Lancaster, *Mathematical Economics*, p. 286.

39. As is evident from the remainder of the passage, Marx is referring here to the "individual" value or price of production—that determined by the new, not yet

generalized method of production—and not to the "social" value or price of production, i.e., the old equilibrium price. The distinction between individual and social value is made in the context of a similar discussion in Vol. I, pp. 316-9.

40. *Capital*, III, pp. 264-5.

41. "Technical changes and the rate of profit," Sec. VII and Appendix V.

42. I am indebted to Locke Anderson for showing me a variant of the proof which follows. I have also benefited from an unpublished proof by Samuel Bowles for a simpler model.

43. Mage, *The Law*, pp. 52-54.

44. *Capital*, I, Chapter XV, Sec. 9.

45. Marx, *Value, Price and Profit* (London: Allen and Unwin, 1899), p. 82.

46. *Capital*, I, p. 417.

47. *Ibid.*, p. 436.

48. This aspect of technical change in capitalism is discussed by Nathan Rosenberg, "The direction of technological change: inducement mechanisms and focusing devices," which is Chapter 6 of his *Perspectives on Technology* (New York: Cambridge University Press, 1976). Jens Christiansen discusses it also in "Marx and the falling rate of profit," *American Economic Review* LXVI (May 1976): 20-26.

49. For example, Gerard Debreu and I. N. Herstein, "Nonnegative square matrices," *Econometrica* XXI (October 1953): 597-607; Lancaster, *Mathematical Economics*, Secs. R7.3 and R7.5; Bródy, *Proportions, Prices and Planning*, Appendix I.

Chapter 8

CONCLUDING REMARKS

This study has had the objective of contributing to a critical understanding of present-day social reality. It has been guided by the two-fold belief that such an understanding requires a critical appropriation of Marx's theory of capitalism and that Habermas's work represents a serious attempt at such an appropriation. Consequently, I have tried to present Habermas's case for his proposed reconstruction of Marxism as strongly as possible and then to evaluate that case in light of a study of Marx's own writings and whatever knowledge I could bring to bear concerning the realities of modern capitalism. With regard to the presentation of Habermas's views, my hope is that by clarifying and rendering more accessible his quite sophisticated and provocative position it will promote fruitful discussion of the issues he raises. As far as actual appraisal of his position is concerned, I have, of course, made no more than a contribution, though I do not wish to underestimate the importance of the conclusions reached, should the argumentation withstand critical scrutiny. In conclusion I wish to draw out some implications of these results and to discuss briefly some of the unresolved issues.

Chapters 5 and 6 contain an interpretation of Marx's critique of political economy which stresses aspects that have often been neglected or

misunderstood, namely the conception of the double character of capitalist production and consequently the analysis of the value form and its
development within capitalism. The claim was explicated and defended
that capital is a social relation of production which must express itself as
the property of a thing, namely as the power of objectified labor to
expand itself at the expense of living labor. The necessity for such an
expression has far-reaching implications. For example, the view is often
attributed to Marx that technological development is politically innocent
or neutral, that the deleterious aspects of capitalism are due merely to a
wrong use of technical capacity and not to a bias in the development of
that capacity. On the other hand, Marx has also frequently been interpreted as espousing a form of technological determinism which sees the
ultimate basis for the generation and solution of social problems as lying in
the process of technological development rather than in the social relations
of production. However, neither of these positions is endorsed by Marx.
While he lays ultimate blame for the evils of capitalism on the relations of
production, he does not see technological development as politically
innocent. Power relations between capital and labor are in part constituted
by the specific technical capacities which are developed as a consequence
of the requirements of value expansion. So long as the relations of
production remain capitalist, there will be a bias against the development
of the capacity to solve certain kinds of problems, even when the means
are available to develop this capacity.

I have tried to support this position and to argue on the basis of it
against Habermas's claim that capitalism places no fetters on the development of the productive forces. I have also argued that Marx's treatment of
the capital-labor relation as an aspect of the production process is not a
reflection of a technocratic tendency in his work but is rather due to his
quite plausible theory that productive and interactive competence are
inextricably intertwined. If these arguments are sound, then Marx is
working with a conceptualization of the process of societal reproduction
which is essential for understanding the dynamics of power relations and
ideology in capitalism. The implication is that in some important respects
Habermas's own conceptualization calls for revision.[1]

But there are epistemological issues associated with Habermas's critique
of Marx which are not explicitly confronted by these arguments. While
Habermas maintains that there are three categorically distinct forms of
inquiry corresponding to three distinct cognitive interests, Marx maintains
at some level a unity-of-science position. As I hope is clear from Chapter 2,
Habermas has developed a systematic theory of knowledge which attributes a distinctive epistemological status to critical social theory. Wellmer

and Habermas claim that this peculiar status is concealed and even denied by Marx's use of analogies with natural science to characterize his approach—in particular by his view that social development is a deterministic process of natural history.[2] A direct investigation of this charge is required before the issue can be settled whether there is any aspect of Marx's work which represents an insensitivity toward or incompatibility with the requirements of the development of interactive competence. But more important than the clarification of Marx's position is the development of an adequate theory of knowledge. In my opinion, part of what is needed in this regard is a more thorough confrontation than has occurred in the literature so far between Habermas's epistemology and the critical discussion of logical empiricism which has been taking place in recent analytic philosophy of science.[3] All too often critics of positivism in the social sciences have disputed a unity-of-science position and advocated a distinctive logic of inquiry for social theory because they are working with a conception of *natural* science which is flawed by a faulty version of empiricism.[4] It would be worthwhile ascertaining whether any of the tenets of logical empiricsm which have been recently discredited infect Habermas's notion of empirical-analytic science in this way.[5]

There is another aspect of Habermas's interpretation of historical materialism which I have not discussed but which has important bearings on the tasks facing Marxism today. Habermas's two standards of progress—the technical and the practical—are transhistorical in the following sense: they are valid for the human species, because they are implicit in the basic activities which make us human, namely social labor and communicative action. Both of these activities take place in "structures of linguistically produced intersubjectivity." It is the presence of such structures which essentially characterizes the human species.[6] The logics of technical and practical rationalization are to be justified within a theory of the *general nature* of such structures, namely the theory of communicative competence, or universal pragmatics. In this way, Habermas uses a concept of the human essence to obtain standards of progress. His main criticism of Marx's historical materialism is that it too narrowly characterizes this essence (i.e., merely as productive activity) and consequently yields inadequate criteria of progress. We have, of course, already dealt with this charge. But what about the philosophical anthropology involved in Habermas's interpretation—the idea that historical progress is to be measured by reference to the realization of historically invariant and indeed anthropologically constitutive values? Is this an accurate interpretation of Marx? More importantly, does critical theory need such an anthropology as a normative basis, as Habermas suggests? With regard to these questions I can only offer a few somewhat tentative remarks, which I hope will help to point the way toward a more definitive treatment.

In Marx's early work, [7] there are certain passages which may plausibly be interpreted as expressing an eschatalogical conception of history as the generation of a human species-subject through the alienated objectification of the human essence and the overcoming of this alienation in communism. According to this conception, Hegel's *Phenomenology* is a mystified theory of this process. Now Habermas is correct, I think, in asserting that in this period of Marx's development he at least sometimes viewed an adequate conceptualization of the general form of human productive activity as yielding a normatively significant logic of development specifying criteria of historical progress. There is some reason to believe, however, that Marx came to abandon this view, at least on the methodological level. In *The German Ideology* Marx was forced to clarify—and perhaps to a certain extent modify—his stance toward Feuerbachian anthropology in response to the criticisms of Stirner. Feuerbach conceived of history as the self-actualization of man as a species being through the overcoming of religious alienation. In Marx's articles in the *Deutsch-Französische Jahrbücher* and in the Paris Manuscripts we see a tracing of this alienation to its roots in economic alienation. However, in some passages history is still conceived of here in a fundamentally Feuerbachian way, viz., as the self-alienation of "man" from his essential powers (as a productive being) and the recovery of this essence in communism. In *The German Ideology,* however, Marx cleary dissociates himself from this conception. He no longer conceives of history as the self-generation of the human species through labor. [8] Among the many passages which indicate the clarification/shift in Marx's position is the following:

> The individuals, who are no longer subject to the division of labor, have been conceived by the philosophers as an ideal, under the name "Man." They have conceived the whole process which we have outlined as the volutionary process of "Man," so that at every historical stage "Man" was substituted for the individuals and shown as the motive force of history. The whole process was thus conceived as a process of the self-estrangement of "Man," and this was essentially due to the fact that the average individual of the later stage was always foisted on to the earlier stage, and the consciousness of a later age on to the individuals of an earlier. Through this inversion, which from the first is an abstract image of the actual conditions, it was possible to transform the whole of history into an evolutionary process of consciousness. [9]

Now the most obvious feature of this new stance is a rejection of the teleology involved in the notion of an ideal species-existence which somehow generates itself. But I would like to suggest that something more is involved: namely, a rejection of the idea of trying to define or measure progress by reference to the realization—however brought about—of a transhistorical essence of the human species. Karl Grün is criticized, for example for having

> an unquestioning faith in the conclusions of German philosophy, as formulated by Feuerbach, viz., that "Man," "pure, true man" is the ultimate purpose of world history, that the human essence . . . is the measure of all things.[10]

There are also indications in the *Grundrisse* that Marx viewed the general form of human productive activity, or production in general, as too abstract to yield criteria of development. A consideration of features of production which are common to all historical epochs can yield nothing by itself about development, Marx says, except "superficial tautologies," such as the statement that "wealth is more easily created where its elements are subjectively and objectively present to a greater degree." The main value which he attributes to the concept of production in general is one of convenience: *"Production in general* is an abstraction, but a rational abstraction in so far as it really brings out the common element and thus saves us repetition."[11] Thus he devotes only nine pages of *Capital* to a consideration of the production process in abstraction from its specific social forms, and he does not seem to be concerned there with trying to provide a logic of development for the productive forces.[12] The point is rather to state those general features of the production process which are relevant for understanding its development in the form of a process of value expansion.

These passages suggest that Marx came to reject the strategy of trying to derive standards of progress from a transhistorical concept of the human essence. Whether he did or not, there seems to be an alternative to Habermas's approach which merits serious attention. Habermas wants to provide an objective justification for the standards which critical theory appeals to in its critique of capitalism. He tries to provide such a justification by anchoring the critique on values which are implicit in (or in Kantian terms, transcendental to) the general form of linguistically produced intersubjectivity which characterizes the human species. That is to say, he tries to base critical theory on anthropologically constitutive and thus transhistorical values. While one cannot rule out a priori that such a project will be successful, there does seem to be a less ambitious option. Suppose that the critical theorist could show that the desirability of replacing society A by society B is a consequence of factual information in conjunction with certain normative standards fundamental to the intersubjectivity of his or her historical epoch. Would not such a demonstration provide the critique with sufficient objectivity? It would not be necessary then to defend the claim that "our first sentence expresses unequivocally the intention of universal and unconstrained consensus."[13] Of course, any anthropologically constitutive standards would also be fundamental to each historical epoch. The question I am raising here is whether it is necessary to seek explicitly to base one's social criticism on such standards. It would be helpful if Habermas said more about why he feels that Marxism must carry this quite heavy burden.

In Chapter 7 I discussed Habermas's claim that because of the institutionalization of "reflexive labor," the law of the tendency of the rate of profit no longer holds in advanced capitalism. I argued that Habermas does not conceive of the law as Marx did, namely as expressing an immanent barrier to capital accumulation, and that if the law indeed had this status in "liberal" capitalism, then it cannot be rendered false in the way Habermas suggests. But although Marx's view was found to have some plausibility, I was not able to present sufficient evidence to warrant attributing this status to the law. The possibility must remain open that although Habermas's interpretation of Marx is incorrect, his theory of reflexive labor incorporates an insight into the dynamics of the profit rate.[14] However, only further politico-economic investigation can settle this question. And such investigation might reveal that although Marx's law is not correct, capital nevertheless does have an immanent barrier that cannot be removed by any sort of state intervention aimed at improving the conditions of capital accumulation. I shall return to this possibility in a moment.

The theory of reflexive labor is Habermas's main criticism of an approach which seeks to apply Marx's value-theoretic analysis to modern capitalism. However, as we have seen, it is not his only criticism, and all of his criticisms are specific versions of the thesis that the value-theoretical conception is inadequate because political and economic phenomena are no longer related to each other as superstructure to base. I wish to conclude with a few remarks on these matters.

The reader will recall[15] that according to Habermas, the collective bargaining process of modern capitalism has a significance which cannot be grasped with value-theoretical concepts. The reason is allegedly that while it is generally possible to analyze price setting in organized markets within the framework of the theory of value by speaking of deviations of price from value due to imperfectly competitive conditions, such a strategy is not possible in the case of the labor market, because the value of labor power is equal to the average wage level "by definition." The idea here is presumably that one is forced by the theory of value to say, for example, that both unorganized migrant farmworkers and strongly unionized workers in the petrochemical industry receive on the average the value of their labor power so that neither is more exploited than the other. One is then forced *conceptually* to give a negative answer to the *empirical* question of whether "class struggle . . . has perhaps had a stabilizing effect only because it has been successful in an economic sense and has visibly altered the rate of exploitation to the advantage of the best organized parts of the working class."[16]

While Habermas's view that the socioeconomic function of collective bargaining is an empirical question should be wholeheartedly endorsed, the argument here about the conceptual apparatus of value theory is unsound. The value of labor power in a given sector is not definitionally equal to the average wage level in that sector, though changes in that level and/or levels in other sectors can produce changes in that value through their effect on the culturally operative conception of minimally adequate living conditions. But the important point is that this historical and moral element entering into the value of labor power provides a *societywide* standard—one which applies to both organized and unorganized sectors of the working class. Consequently, apart from training costs and other job-related requirements which could produce calculable differentials, the value of labor power is the same across sectors. Consequently it is an empirically meaningful question whether some sectors of the working class are getting more than the value of their labor power and others less. Thus the conceptual apparatus of value theory does not rule out a priori that the collective bargaining process has had the function and effect suggested by Habermas.

Habermas' remaining criticism[17] of the value-theoretical "conceptual strategy" is that it cannot perceive a new sort of susceptibility to crisis in modern capitalsim. The reasoning is as follows: The state's market-tampering activities obviously cannot be justified by reference to the fairness of the market. In principle, these economic activities thus become matters for public deliberations, and the door is thereby opened for people to make use of the institutions of political democracy to demand that state intervention be directed toward the accommodation of legitimate needs whose satisfaction was formerly the exclusive province of the market. Such demands on the part of the population at large would overtax the ability of the state to produce and maintain conditions of capital accumulation. The state must therefore conduct its economic crisis-managing activities in such a way that it retains mass loyalty *without* mass participation in the process of political decision-making. The fact that the door to this process is open to the population, by virtue of both the collapse of the ideology of fair exchange and the existence of formally democratic political instituions, means that modern capitalism faces a new sort of legitimation problem. The classical Marxian approach is incapable of perceiving this problem, because it is constrained to view bourgeois democracy as a mere superstructure to class domination in the economic sphere and hence as not a source of crisis:

> Once again, a dogmatic conceptual strategy, which admits bourgeois democracy only as a superstructure of capitalist class domination, misses the specific problem. To the extent that the state no longer represents merely the superstructure of an unpolitical class relationship, the formally democratic means for procuring legitimation prove to be peculiarly restrictive. . . . As long as the capitalist economic system begot of itself a viable ideology, a comparable legitimation problem . . . could not arise.[18]

In my opinion, Habermas's hypotheses pertaining to the susceptibility of modern capitalism to this type of legitimation crisis may represent the most important part of his social-theoretic work and may well constitute crucial insights into the dynamics of modern capitalism. Of course, more research is needed to determine whether the structures of the political insitutions in modern capitalist societies would in fact permit insoluble legitimation difficulties to arise. But research along these lines is quite important, as are Habermas's inquiries into the conditions of reproduction of motivational syndromes of privatism which help to secure political abstinence. Once again, however, I am skeptical of Habermas's claim about the approach of the critique of political economy. There seems to be a certain unclarity or ambiguity in his stance toward this approach. Sometime he seems to be arguing that it is important to do *more* than develop the critique of political economy, because there are important sources of potential crisis which are external to the capital relation. This position seems absolutely correct, and it provides a justification for much of his research. On the other hand, sometimes he seems to be arguing that we need to *abandon* the development of the critique of political economy, because its concepts are *unfit* to contribute to an understanding of modern capitalism. This seems to be his view about collective bargaining, for example. It is this position which seems incorrect to me. Of course, a lot hinges on what we take to be the approach of the critique of political economy. Here our earlier analysis seems to have some relevant implications. We saw in our earlier discussion of the dynamics of capital accumulation[19] that Marx was concerned to show that capital has an immanent barrier, but that such a claim was not to be construed as a denial of the causal relevance of factors external to capital in the occurrence of crises. Indeed, it is Marx's position that the actual development of capitalism is always due to external as well as internal factors. To demonstrate an immanent barrier is to show that the system *would* eventually break down *even if* external conditions *were* optimal; it does not presuppose or assert that external conditions actually *are* optimal. For this reason, state intervention does not render the critique of political economy conceptually unsuitable for modern capitalism. Marx's approach does not conceptually rule out that formally democratic institutions could intensify legitimation problems in the manner Habermas suggests; it is just that this eventuality, important as it is, is not appealed to in the attempt to show that capital has an immanent barrier.

The present study suggests that whether or not capital has such a barrier is still very much an open and important question. It is not a question which can be decided merely by citing the fact of state intervention in the economy, but only by pursuing the sort of economic investigation which Marx began. On the contrary, the scope of possible successful intervention itself hinges importantly on the answer to this question. While a negative answer would not mean that capitalism will be free of economic crisis, it would have implications for the sort of critical stance which should be taken toward state policy. The weight of socialist criticism would have to be carried by arguments which allowed that there is no barrier in the structure of capital per se to successful crisis management. Indeed, this is Habermas's position. On the other hand, a positive answer would not at all render insignificant potential sources of crisis outside of the capital relation. It could even be a factor in bringing about a legitimation crisis of the sort Habermas envisages, for it would provide a basis for arguing that modern capitalism, including its crisis-manager state apparatus, is incapable of solving the problems that face it and consequently cannot be expected to meet people's legitimate needs.

NOTES

1. The argumentation of Chapters 5 and 6 can be seen as spelling out and supporting the following sort of position, expressed by Richard J. Bernstein in a footnote: "Habermas' criticism of Marx presupposes the validity of the categorial distinction between work and interaction. Habermas is accusing Marx of merging

what ought to be sharply distinguished. But one can turn Marx against Habermas, for Marx shows the dangers that can result from making such a dichotomy. . . . Rather than charging Marx with some sort of category mistake, a more penetrating interpretation would question the very categorial distinction that Habermas takes to be fundamental."*The Restructuring of Social and Political Theory* (New York: Harcourt Brace Jovanovich, 1976), p. 260, n. 30.

2. They are particularly disturbed by Marx's approval of a characterization of his method by a Russian reviewer of *Capital*. See *Capital*, I, pp. 17-19; Habermas, *Knowledge and Human Interests*, p. 46; Wellmer, *Critical Theory of Society*, p. 68n.

3. For a very useful historical account of this discussion, see the Introduction and Afterward to *The Structure of Scientific Theories*, ed. by Frederick Suppe (Urbana: University of Illinois Press, 1977). A provocative new approach which has recently arisen out of the discussion is that of Larry Laudan, *Progress and Its Problems* (Berkeley: University of California Press, 1977). Nikolaus Lobkowicz asserts in a review of *Knowledge and Human Interests* that in Habermas's criticism of positivism he is "tilting at windmills generally, for the positivism he fights is no longer defended even by the survicors of the Vienna Circle" ("Interest and objectivity," *Philosophy of the Social Sciences* II (1972): 200). Habermas discusses his views in connection with recent analytic philosophy of science in "a postscript to *Knowledge and Human Interests.*"

4. Claims that Marx is not an empiricist often are faulty in this regard. On this matter see Richard Henry Hudelson, *Marx's Conception of Social Science* (Ph.D. dissertation, University of Michigan, 1977).

5. A good starting point for such an investigation would be an essay by Mary Hesse, "In defense of objectivity," *Proceedings of the British Academy* LVIII (1972): 275-292.

6. *Legitimation Crisis*, p. 10.

7. The following reflections on Marx's development were influenced in part by Jindřich Zelený, *Die Wissenschaftslogik und "Das Kapital,"* trans. by Peter Bollhagen (Frankfurt: Europäische Verlagsanstalt, 1973), Pt. II, and Renate Damus, "Habermas und der 'heimliche Positivismus' bei Marx," *Sozialistische Politik* I (December 1969): 22-46.

8. Thus unless there is a reversion in Marx's position, Habermas is mistaken in interpreting the controversial passage from the *Grundrisse* which we discussed on pp. 117-22 as an expression of this view of history. See *Knowledge and Human Interests*, pp. 47-51.

9. Marx and Engels, *The German Ideology* (Moscow: Progress Publishers, 1968), p. 86. See also pp. 49-50, 259.

10. Ibid., p. 578.

11. *Grundrisse*, pp. 87, 85.

12. *Capital* I, Ch. VII, Sec. 1.

13. *Knowledge and Human Interests*, p. 314.

14. I am referring to Habermas's theory as explicated in this study. An earlier version seems to contain confusions between wealth and value, involving a misguided attempt to make value serve as an index of real output. See *Theory and Practice*, pp. 227-31 and p. 302, n. 45.

15. See Ch. 4, pp. 63-5.

16. *Legitimation Crisis*, p. 57.

17. See Ch. 4, pp. 65-8.

18. *Legitimation Crisis*, p. 58.

19. Ch. 7, pp. 126-7.

BIBLIOGRAPHY

Apel, Karl-Otto, ed. *Sprachpragmatik und Philosophie.* Frankfurt: Suhrkamp, 1976.
Aristotle. *Nicomachean Ethics. The Basic Works of Aristotle.* Edited by Richard McKeon. New York: Random House, 1941.
———. *Nicomachean Ethics.* Translated by Martin Ostwald. Indianapolis: Bobbs-Merrill, 1962.
———. *Metaphysics. The Basic Works of Aristotle.* Edited by Richard McKeon. New York: Random House, 1941.
———. *Posterior Analytics. The Basic Works of Aristotle.* Edited by Richard McKeon. New York: Random House, 1941.
Ashby, W. Ross. *Design for a Brain.* London: Chapman and Hall, 1960.
———. *An Introduction to Cybernetics.* London: Chapman and Hall, 1956.
Bader, Veit-Michael: Berger, Johannes; Ganssmann, Heiner; Hagelstange, Thomas; Hoffmann, Burkhard; Kratke, Michael; Krais, Beate; Kürschner, Lor; and Strehl, Rudiger. *Krise und Kapitalismus bei Marx.* 2 vols. n.p.: Europäische Verlagsanstalt, 1975.
Bergmann, Gustav. *Philosophy of Science.* Madison: University of Wisconsin Press, 1957.
———. "Reduction." *Current Trends in Psychology and the Behavioral Sciences.* Pittsburgh: University of Pittsburgh Press, 1954.
Bernstein, Richard. *The Restructuring of Social and Political Theory.* New York: Harcourt Brace Jovanovich, 1976.
Bródy, András. *Proportions, Prices and Planning.* Budapest: Akadémiai Kiadó, 1970. Amsterdam and London: North Holland, 1970. New York: American Elsevier, 1970.
Buck, Robert Creighton, and Buck, Ellen F. *Advanced Calculus.* New York: McGraw-Hill, 1965.
Carnap, Rudolf. *Philosophical Foundations of Physics.* New York: Basic Books, 1966.
Christiansen, Jens. "Marx and the falling rate of profit." *American Economic Review* LXVI (May 1976): 20-26.
Colletti, Lucio. *From Rousseau to Lenin.* Translated by John Merrington and Judith White. New York: Monthly Review Press, 1972.
Commoner, Barry. *The Closing Circle.* New York: Alfred A. Knopf, 1971.
———. *The Poverty of Power.* New York: Alfred A. Knopf, 1976.
Dallmayr, Fred R. and McCarthy, Thomas A., eds. *Understanding and Social Theory.*

Notre Dame: University of Notre Dame Press, 1977.

Damus, Renate. "Habermas und der 'heimliche Positivismus' bei Marx." *Sozialistische Politkik* 1, 4 (December 1969): 22-46.

Debreu, Gerard and Herstein, I. N. "Nonnegative square matrices." *Econometrica* XXI (October 1953): 597-607.

Elkind, David. "Egocentrism in adolescence." *Child Development* XXXVIII (1967): 1025-34.

Fisk, Milton. "Rate of profit and class struggle." *Radical Philosophers Newsjournal* 5 (August 1975): 1-37.

Flood, Tony. "Jürgen Habermas's critique of Marxism." *Science and Society* XLI (Winter 1977-78): 448-64.

Gendron, Bernard and Holmstrom, Nancy. "Marx, machinery and alienation." *Research in Philosophy and Technology* III. JAI Press, forthcoming.

Gillman, Joseph. *The Falling Rate of Profit.* London: Dennis Dobson, 1957.

Habermas, Jürgen. *Erkenntnis and Interesse.* Frankfurt: Suhrkamp, 1973.

–––. *Knowledge and Human Interests.* Translated by Jeremy J. Shapiro. Boston: Beacon Press, 1971.

–––. *Legitimation Crisis.* Translated by Thomas McCarthy. Boston, Beacon Press, 1975.

–––. *Legitimationsprobleme im Spätkapitalismus.* Frankfurt: Suhrkamp, 1973.

–––. "Moral development and ego identity." *Telos* 24 (Summer 1975): 41-55.

–––. "On social identity." *Telos* 19 (Spring 1974): 91-104.

–––. "On systematically distorted communication." *Inquiry* XIII (Autumn 1970): 205-18.

–––. "A postscript to *Knowledge and Human Interests.*" *Philosophy of the Social Sciences* III (1973): 157-89.

–––. "Stumpf gewordene Waffen aus dem Arsenal der Gegenauflklärung." *Briefe zur Verteidigung der Republik.* Edited by Freimut Duve, Heinrich Böll, and Klaus Staeck. Reinbek bei Hamburg: Rowohlt, 1977.

–––. *Technik und Wissenschaft als "Ideologie."* Frankfurt: Suhrkamp, 1968.

–––. "A test for popular justice: the accusations against the intellectuals." *New German Critique* 12 (Fall 1977): 11-13.

–––. *Theorie und Praxis.* Frankfurt: Suhrkamp, 1971.

–––. *Theory and Practice.* Translated by John Viertel. Boston: Beacon Press, 1973.

–––. *Toward a Rational Society.* Translated by Jeremy J. Shapiro. Boston: Beacon Press, 1970.

–––. "Toward a reconstruction of historical materialism." *Theory and Society* II (1975): 287-300.

–––. "Towards a theory of communicative competence." *Inquiry* XIII (Winter 1970): 360-75.

–––. "Der Universalitätsanspruch der Hermeneutik." Karl-Otto Apel et al. *Hermeneutic und Ideologiekritik.* Frankfurt: Suhrkamp, 1971.

–––. "Wahrheitstheorien." *Wirklichkeit und Reflexion: Walter Schulz zum 60. Geburtstag.* Edited by Helmut Fahrenbach. Pfullingen: Gunther Neske, 1973.

–––. "Was heisst Universalpragmatik?" *Sprachpragmatik und Philosophie.* Edited by Karl-Otto Apel. Frankfurt: Suhrkamp, 1976.

–––. *Zur Logik der Sozialwissenschaften.* Frankfurt: Suhrkamp, 1971.

–––. *Zur Rekonstruktion des Historischen Materialismus.* Frankfurt: Suhrkamp, 1976.

–––, and Frankel, Boris. "Habermas talking: an interview," *Theory and Society* I (1974): 37-58.

———, and Luhmann, Niklas. *Theorie der Gesellschaft oder Sozialtechologie—was leistet die Systemforschung?* Frankfurt: Suhrkamp, 1971.

Hegel, G.W.F. *The Logic of Hegel.* Translated from *The Encyclopedia of the Philosophical Sciences* by William Wallace. London: Oxford University Press, 1892.

———. *Die Wissenschaft der Logik.* Part I of *Enzyklopädie der philosophischen Wissenschaften im Grundrisse. Werke in zwanzig Banden.* Edited by Eva Moldenhauer and Karl Markus Michel. Frankfurt: Suhrkamp, 1970.

Hempel, Carl G. *Fundamentals of Concept Formation in Empirical Science.* Vol. II, No. 7 of *International Encyclopedia of United Science.* Edited by Otto Neurath. Chicago: University of Chicago Press, 1952.

Hermeneutics and critical theory." Symposium in *Cultural Hermeneutics,* II (February 1975), 307-90.

Hesse, Mary. "In defence of objectivity." *Proceedings of the British Academy* LVIII (1972): 275-292.

Hodgson, Geoff. "The theory of the falling rate of profit." *New Left Review* 84 (March-April 1974): 55-82.

Holländer, Heinz. "Das Gesetz des tendenziellen Falls der Profitrate." *Mehrwert* 6 (June 1974): 105-35.

Horkheimer, Max. *Critical Theory.* Translated by Matthew J. O'Donnell *et al.* New York: Herder and Herder, 1972.

———, and Adorno, Theodor W. *Dialectic of Enlightenment.* Translated by John Cumming. New York: Herder and Herder, 1972.

Howard, Dick. "Moral development and ego identity: a clarification." *Telos* 27 (Spring 1976): 176-82.

Hudelson, Richard Henry. *Marx's Conception of Social Science.* Ph.D. Dissertation. University of Michigan, 1977.

Jay, Martin. *The Dialectical Imagination.* Boston: Little, Brown, 1973.

Kant, Immanuel. *Critique of Pure Reason.* Translated by Norman Kemp Smith. New York: St. Martin's, 1929.

Kellner, Douglas. "The Frankfurt School revisited: a critique of Martin Jay's *The Dialectical Imagination.*" *New German Critique* IV (1975): 131-52.

Lancaster, Kelvin. *Mathematical Economics.* New York: Macmillan, 1968.

Laudan, Larry. *Progress and Its Problems.* Berkeley: University of California Press, 1977.

Linder, Marc. *Reification and the Consciousness of the Critics of Political Economy: Studies in the Development of Marx' Theory of Value.* Ph.D. dissertation, Princeton University, 1973. Published in Copenhagen by Rhodos International Science and Art Publishers, 1975.

Lobkowicz, Nikolaus, "Interest and objectivity." *Philosophy of the Social Sciences* II (1972): 193-210.

Lukács, Georg. *History and Class Consciousness.* Translated by Rodney Livingstone. Cambridge, Mass.: MIT Press, 1971.

McCarthy, T[homas] A. "A theory of communicative competence." *Philosophy of the Social Sciences* III (1973): 135-56.

Mage, Shane. *The Law of the Falling Tendency of the Rate of Profit.* Ph.D. dissertation, Columbia University, 1963.

Marcuse, Herbert. *Negations: Essays in Critical Theory.* Translated by Jeremy J. Shapiro. Boston: Beacon Press, 1968.

———. *One Dimensional Man.* Boston: Beacon Press, 1964.

Marx, Karl. *Capital*. Edited by Frederick Engels. 3 vols. New York: International Publishers, 1967.

———. *A Contribution to the Critique of Political Economy*. Moscow: Progress Publishers, 1970.

———. *Economic and Philosophical Manuscripts of 1844*. Marx, Karl, and Engeles, Frederick. *Collected Works*. Vol. III. New York: International Publishers, 1975.

———. *Grundrisse*. Translated by Martin Nicolaus. Baltimore: Penguin, 1973.

———. *Grundrisse der Kritik der politischen Ökonomie*. Berlin (E.): Dietz, 1953.

———. *Das Kapital*, Vol. I. Marx, Karl and Engels, Friedrich. *Werke*. Vol. XXIII. Berlin: Dietz, 1962.

———. *Das Kapital*, Vol. III. Marx, Karl and Engels, Friedrich. *Werke*. Vol. XXV. Berlin: Dietz, 1964.

———. Letter to Engels of August 24, 1867. Marx, Karl and Engels, Friedrich. *Werke*. Vol. XXXI. Berlin: Dietz, 1965.

———. *Letter to Engels of January 8, 1868. Marx, Karl and Engels, Friedrich. Werke*. Vol. XXXII. Berlin: Dietz, 1965.

———. *The Poverty of Philosophy*. New York: International Publishers, 1963.

———. *Resultate des unmittelbaren Produktionsprozesses*. Frankfurt: Verlag Neue Kritik, 1974.

———. *Theories of Surplus Value*, Part I. Translated by Emile Burns. Moscow: Progress Publishers, 1963.

———. *Theories of Surplus Value*, Part III. Translated by Jack Cohen and S.W. Ryazanskaya. Moscow: Progress Publishers, 1971.

———. *Zur Kritik der politischen Ökonomie*. Marx, Karl and Engels, Friedrich. *Werke*. Vol. XIII. Berlin: Dietz, 1964.

———, and Engels, Friedrich. *Die deutsche Ideologie*. *Werke*. Vol. III. Berlin: Dietz, 1962.

———. *The German Ideology*. Moscow: Progress Publishers, 1968.

———. *Studienausgabe*. Edited by I. Fetscher. Vol. II. Frankfurt, 1966.

Mayr, Ernst. *Animal Species and Evolution*. Cambridge Mass.: Harvard University Press, 1963.

Medio, Alfredo. "Profits and surplus-value: appearance and reality in capitalist production." *A Critique of Economic Theory*. Edited by E.K. Hunt and Jessie G. Schwartz. Baltimore: Penguin, 1972.

Morishima, Michio. *Marx's Economics*. New York: Cambridge University Press, 1973.

Müller, Wolfgang. "Habermas und die 'Anwendbarkeit' der 'Arbeitswerttheorie.' " *Sozialistische Politkik* I (April 1969): 39-53.

———, and Neusüss, Christel. "Die Sozialstaatsillusion und der Widerspruch von Lohnarbeit und Kapital." *Probleme des Klassenkampfs*, Sonderheft 1 (June 1971): 7-70. A translation appears in *Telos* 25 (Fall 1975): 13-98.

Nielsen, Kai. "The political relevance of Habermas." *Radical Philosophers News-journal* VII (August 1976): 1-11.

O'Connor, James. *The Fiscal Crisis of the State*. New York: St. Martin's, 1973.

Okishio, Nobuo. "Technical changes and the rate of profit." *Kobe University Economic Review* VII (1961): 85-99.

Palmer, R. *Hermeneutics*. Evanston, Ill.: Northwestern University Press, 1968.

Radnitzky, Gerard. *Contemporary Schools of Metascience*. Chicago: Henry Regnery, 1973.

Rosdolsky, Roman. *The Making of Marx's Capital*. New York: Urizen, 1977.

–––. *Zur Entstehungsgeschichte des Marxschen "Kapital."* 2 vols. Frankfurt: Europäische Verlagsanstalt, 1968.

Rosenberg, Nathan. *Perspectives on Technology.* New York: Cambridge University Press, 1976.

Rudner, Richard S. *Philosophy of Social Science.* Englewood Cliffs, N.J.: Prentice-Hall, 1966.

Schefold, Bertram. "Different forms of technical progress." *Economic Journal* LXXXVI (December 1976): 806-819.

Slater, Phil. *Origin and Significance of the Frankfurt School.* London, Henley and Boston: Routledge and Kegan Paul, 1977.

Stace, W. I. *The Philosophy of Hegel.* New York: Dover, 1955.

Steedman, Ian. *Marx after Sraffa.* London: New Left Books, 1977.

Suppe, Frederick, ed. *The Structure of Scientific Theories.* Urbana: University of Illinois Press, 1977.

Therborn, Göran, "Jurgen Habermas: a new eclecticism." *New Left Review* 67 (May-June 1971): 69-83.

Wellmer, Albrecht. *Critical Theory of Society.* Translated by John Cumming. New York: Seabury Press, 1974.

–––. *Kritische Gesellschaftstheorie und Positivismus.* Frankfurt: Suhrkamp, 1969.

Wilson, Edward O. *Sociobiology.* Cambridge, Mass.: The Belnap Press of Harvard University Press, 1975.

Wright, Georg Henrik von. *Explanation and Understanding.* Ithaca, N.Y.: Cornell University Press, 1971.

Zeitschrift für Sozialforschung, I-VIII (1932-9).

Zelený, Jindřich. *Die Wissenschaftslogik und "Das Kapital."* Translated by Peter Bollhagen. Frankfurt: Europäische Verlagsanstalt, 1973.

INDEX

alienation, 87-88, 92, 104, 106-109, 110-112, 114
Apel, Karl-Otto, 35
Aristotle, 17-20, 34
Ashby, W. Ross, 44

base and superstructure, 12, 56-59, 67, 166
Bernstein, E., 73, 93n2
Butler, Samuel, 80

capital, 90-93
  as a specific social form of production, 90-93, 101-109
capital accumulation
  immanent barrier to, 14, 126-127, 143-145, 164-167
  Marx vs. Habermas on, 126-127
capitalism
  advanced vs. liberal, 56-58
  Marx's general characterization of, 90-92
Chomsky, Noam, 35
classical political economy, 82, 89
cognitive interests, see interests, cognitive
collective bargaining, 63-65, 164-165
commodities, Marx's conception of, 79-90
communicative action
  defined, 18-19, 36n7
  vs. discourse, 23
  Marx and, 69, 98-101, 122
  and production, 42-43, 72, 99-100
  pure, 26
  and socialization, 42-43
communicative competence, theory of, 31-35, 42, 161-164
correctness, 23, 34, 52
critical theory

as a synthesis of hermeneutic and empirical analytic approaches, 24-31
inadequacies in Habermas's view of, 12-13, 109-117, 159-161
Marx and, 30, 68-75, 88-89, 92-93, 101, 109-112, 114, 116, 117-122, 159-161
philosophical foundations of, 31-35, 50-52, 161-164
critique of political economy
  as critical theory, 30, 68-69, 109-117, 124n38
  fundamentals of, 79-92
  and historical materialism, 97-122

dialectic of enlightenment, 71-72
Dilthey, Wilhelm, 21, 26
discourse
  defined, 23
  and social learning, 47-48, 111
  therapeutic, 31-33

economic crisis, 49, 59, 62, 144-145, 153, 164-167
emancipatory interest, see interests, cognitive
empirical-analytic inquiry
  as a method in social theory, 17-23
  critical theory and, 24-31, 160-161
  Marx and, 68-75, 160-161
ethical cognitivism, 25, 33-35, 37n30, 50-52, 74
ethical naturalism, 37n30
exchange value, 80-82

fetishism
  of capital, 92-93, 110-111
  of commodities, 88-90, 110
Feuerbach, Ludwig, 162

forces of production, see productive
forces
Frankfurt School, 13, 17, 71, 114

Galilean paradigm for social science, 20,
25
Grün, Karl, 163

Hegel, G. W. F., 68-69, 102, 162
hermeneutics
as a method in social theory, 17-23
and critical theory, 24-31
historical materialism, 33, 42
criticism of Marx's formulation of,
22-13, 68-75, 97-101
in Marx, 97-122
Hobbes, Thomes, 20-24
Hume, David, 34, 37n30

ideal speech situation, 27-28
ideology
compared to rationalization, 28-31
of fair exchange, 30, 57, 65-67,
116-117, 124n38, 165
technocratic, 70-75, 101, 106-107,
110-111, 114, 160
Institut für Sozialforschung, 17
instrumental action, 18, 36n7
interaction, symbolically mediated
defined, 18-19, 36n7
vs. discourse, 23
Marx and, 69, 98-101, 122
and production, 42-43, 72, 99-100
pure, 26
and socialization, 42-43
interests
cognitive
emancipatory, 32-35
practical, 20-22, 24-26
technical, 20-22, 24-25
generalizable, 29, 33

Kant, Immanuel, 34, 163
Keynesian policies, 57
knowledge-guiding interests, see interests, cognitive

labor power,
as a commodity, 90
value of, 63-64, 90, 164-165
legitimation crisis, 49, 57-58, 65-68,
165-167
Leninism, 73
Lukács, Georg, 124n47

Mage, Shane, 151
money, Marx's theory of, 89-90
naturalistic fallacy, 52
see also ethical naturalism

O'Connor, James, 62
Okishio, Nobuo, 129, 150-152
organic composition of capital, 13,
156n19

philology, 21, 27
positivism, 11, 97-98, 160-161
practical interest, see interests, cognitive
practical rationalization, 12-13, 43-44,
46-52, 68-75, 100, 111-112, 121-122
principle of organization, 45-46, 50
of liberal capitalism, 56
production
Habermas's concept of, 42-44, 68,
98-101, 111, 122, 160
Marx's concept of, 79-82-88, 90-92,
98-109
productive forces
characterizations of, 42-44, 112-113,
124n33
development of, 13, 43-44, 46-52,
68-72, 108-114, 121-122,
139-140, 160, 163
progress, historical, 50-52
purposive-rational action
defined, 18-19
and empirical-analytic inquiry, 20-22
and Marx, 122
and production, 42-43, 68, 122

ratio of dead to living labor
defined, 131
and organic composition of capital,
156n19
sectoral, 133
secular rise of, as functionally
necessary to capitalism, 143-145
and technical change, 131-143
real wages
and capitalist development, 151
and the rate of profit, 149-152
and technical change, 152
real subsumption of labor under capital,
101-109
Habermas and, 109-117
vs. merely formal subsumption,
102-103
reduction, 98-99
reflection, 32, 68-69
reflective labor, 59-62, 164
Ricardo, David, 126

Schumpeter, J. A., 74
scientific revolution, 20, 47
self-reflection, see reflection
social integration, 49
socialization

ABOUT THE AUTHOR

JULIUS SENSAT, Jr. is Assistant Professor of Philosophy at
the University of Wisconsin—Milwaukee. He did his graduate
work at Princeton University and the University of Texas at
Austin, and he has taught at the University of Michigan and
the University of California, Los Angeles. He is a junior author
of Marc Linder's *Anti-Samuelson* (New York: Urizen Books,
1977).